THE GIFT OF NOT BELONGING

THE GIFT OF NOT BELONGING

HOW OUTSIDERS THRIVE IN A WORLD OF JOINERS

DR. RAMI KAMINSKI

New York Boston London

Little, Brown Spark
Hachette Book Group
1290 Avenue of the Americas
New York, NY 10104
littlebrownspark.com

First Edition: June 2025

Little, Brown Spark is an imprint of Little, Brown and Company, a division of Hachette Book Group, Inc. The Little, Brown Spark name and logo are trademarks of Hachette Book Group, Inc.

The publisher is not responsible for websites (or their content) that are not owned by the publisher.

The Hachette Speakers Bureau provides a wide range of authors for speaking events. To find out more, go to hachettespeakersbureau.com or email HachetteSpeakers@hbgusa.com.

Print book interior design by Jeff Stiefel

ISBN 9780316576086 (hc) / 9780316596497 (int'l pb)
LCCN 2024949101

Printing 1, 2025

LSC-C

Printed in the United States of America

For Maya

Contents

Contents

THE GIFT OF NOT
BELONGING

Introduction

H ow can I be of help to you?"

"What do you think should be your treatment goals?"

These are usually the first questions I ask when I sit down with a new patient. Most people do not have answers to these questions at the outset, which is expected. I'm not looking to get an answer but rather to emphasize that the patient is in charge of what happens next because what we are dealing with is their own life. I often say, "You are the captain, and this is your ship. I am a navigator you've hired to assist you in charting a course through a sea unfamiliar to you but familiar to me since I've crossed it numerous times." No matter how that journey unfolds, my desired goal for my patients is always the same. At the end of our work together, I want them to be happy that they are who they are.

On the surface, that might seem like a modest goal. But we humans know how difficult it is. So many of us live our lives yearning to look like someone else, to have what another has, or even to be someone else. Aspiring for something is not a problem in itself. However, since we usually aspire for something we consider better than what we have, many of us are left with a poor opinion of who we already are and the lives we already live.

Sometimes, the yearning to be less like ourselves and more like someone else is rooted in envy, or ambition, or the genuine desire to better ourselves. But often, when a patient comes to me seeking transformation, further inspection reveals that what they truly want is to be a person who is liked and accepted: someone who fits in. They have learned that belonging is both a virtue and a goal that should be shared by all human beings, when in fact, belonging is neither: belonging is merely a feeling; it does not exist in reality as a tangible thing.

Therein unfolds one of humanity's great difficulties: how to manage the fact that each of us is a unique individual constantly chasing a feeling that is directly at odds with their individuality.

In my forty-plus years as a practicing physician and psychiatrist, my interests have taken me from a remote area in the Sinai desert, where I worked as the sole physician treating nomadic Bedouin tribes, to running the schizophrenia unit at Mount Sinai Hospital in New York City (from one Sinai to the other), to being appointed the medical director for operations in the New York agency that runs all aspects of mental health care in the state. I've taught students and residents, treated patients in the community and in academic medical centers (Mount Sinai and then Columbia Presbyterian), conducted clinical and pharmacological research, and always maintained an active private practice.

All the while, I have continued to develop my original therapeutic philosophy.

In my private practice in Manhattan I have worked with numerous people from all walks of life. Among them are world leaders, renowned performing artists, and professionals at the top of their fields. Many of them come to me seeking to understand why they feel so disconnected from the people closest and most familiar to them—friends, colleagues, and even family. Over the course of our sessions, it often emerges that they have gone through life feeling incapable of fitting in. When around others, they are always an observer but never an actual participant, and regardless of the group of people they are with, they never feel like they truly belong. While most people forge a sense of self in their relation to others—they identify first and foremost as a husband or a mother, a teacher or a leader—these patients experience life outside the communal hive.

The vast majority of these people have no psychiatric diagnosis. They are not neurodivergent or on the autism spectrum. They aren't socially maladjusted or even socially anxious. So why do they struggle so much with fitting in? In rare cases, their social difficulties stem from shyness or introversion. Occasionally, they are a result of having been marginalized or "othered" based on race, gender expression, or disability. But for most of them, there is another entirely different explanation. After many years spent observing and researching these characteristics, I've discovered that they are rooted in a particular and previously unrecognized trait that is present in people of every ethnicity, race, and gender from all parts of the world: one hallmarked by the lack of a communal impulse or, in other words, an innate inability to feel like they belong. It's a way of being I understand viscerally.

I, too, spent the early part of my life wondering why I always felt so different from those around me. I was not shunned or rejected. I had friends, I was funny, and by all accounts, I was a popular kid. I liked school. I wasn't shy, introverted, or socially anxious, and I enjoyed running through the endless maze of backyards and buildings in the city where I grew up. On the outside, I seemed like a happy, well-adjusted kid. But on the inside, I felt like an ugly duckling. I was part of several different friend groups throughout my childhood, yet I never felt like I truly belonged in any of them. Whatever wall separated me from the others was invisible. No matter how popular I was, I always felt like an outsider.

Group activities that all my friends happily participated in—sports teams, day camps, and camping, what most kids looked forward to—were very unpleasant for me for no apparent reason. But I feared that voicing these feelings would make me seem strange or abnormal, so I pretended to look forward to them just as much as all the other kids. Paradoxically, I was a popular loner who learned to fashion a cool, outgoing facade. To others, my jovial personality seemed effortless. It was anything but.

This charade became increasingly hard to sustain with the onset of puberty. On top of the typical adolescent emotional tsunami, I was besieged by confusion and frustration about my inability to care about what everyone else did. I desperately wanted to enjoy the affinity my social group displayed; I wanted to share the feeling of "togetherness," the gossip, the tales of sexual conquest, the obsession with sports teams, the encyclopedic knowledge of every Rolling Stones song ever written, and everything else that my peers—both male and female—seemed to desire. But I could not muster any genuine excitement or interest in any of it. I preferred authentic conversation—the exchange of confidences and truths, rather than superficial small talk and bravado—but as teenagers do, I faked what seemed required of me. I learned the names of soccer players, went to parties, dressed like all the cool guys, and let my hair grow long. When the conversation turned to anything even mildly controversial, from politics to which girl in the class was prettiest to what we all thought of the latest blockbuster movie, I would wait to see what the group consensus was and go along with it, even though I almost always disagreed.

Outwardly, I was no different from the other kids in the progressive school I attended. My discomfort was internal. I did not dare share it with anyone. My around-the-clock performance may have been Oscar worthy, but it left me feeling empty and exhausted.

Then, when I was in my twenties, something changed. My labored efforts to demonstrate easygoing kinship with my peers grew unsustainable. As an undergraduate and then a medical student, I had a rigorous course load, and spending my limited free time on activities I did not enjoy became less and less appealing. I craved opportunities to speak my mind and nurture close one-on-one friendships, unencumbered by group dynamics. I no longer felt I needed the group's approval to validate my existence, and I no longer cared to let the majority opinion influence my views or decision-making. I decided it was time to stop performing.

Around this time, I also realized that my lifelong lack of connection to what moves and motivates groups of people made me an exceptionally keen observer, always seeking to decipher behaviors that I found perplexing. Unencumbered by any authentic desire to follow the flock, I learned to connect powerfully to individual people rather than abide by tribal norms that suppress deep, empathic connections and isolate us from those deemed outsiders. Because I always felt an arm's length away from the collective, I could see its members as individuals, each with their unique emotional responses, patterns, and personalities. I now understood that in constantly (if silently) questioning the group consensus, I had become an outside-the-box thinker who approached problems from new angles that others couldn't or didn't want to see. In addition, my disinterest in most popular activities, trends, and hobbies allowed me to throw myself fully, and with laser-like focus, into my interests and studies.

In other words, this aspect of my personality—this "non-belonging"—that had so baffled my younger self was the very thing that enabled me to forge a successful and deeply fulfilling career in psychiatry. I was not an ugly duckling, nor was I a swan. I was another kind of bird altogether. After a bruising passage through adolescence, this discovery exposed a thrilling possibility: instead of following the flock, I could chart my own trajectory.

The more I observed and studied these personality characteristics—in myself, in others like me whom I encountered, and in those patients for whom no known diagnosis could explain the sense of otherness they felt—the more I was able to isolate a distinct set of traits that we all shared. As I started writing about what I discovered, I searched for a word to describe people like this—which, of course, included myself.

Most people are familiar with Carl Jung's concepts of extrovert ("one who faces outward") and introvert ("one who faces inward"): terms that have earned a recognizable place in the language of popular psychology. But people like me face neither inward nor outward: our fundamental orientation is defined by the fact that it is rarely the same direction that everyone else is facing. That is how I came up with the term "otrovert." In Spanish (etymologically inherited from Latin), "otro" means "other" and "vert" means "direction." Quite literally, otrovert means "one who is facing a different direction."

Our society puts a tremendous amount of emphasis on the benefits of community and belonging. This is logical, especially at a time when more people are reporting suffering the profound effects of loneliness, alienation, and disconnection than ever before.

That social connection confers a variety of health and mental health benefits is well documented. But connection is not the same as belonging, despite the fact that the two are often equated in our society. When we say that we "belong," we are saying that we feel at one with a group, be it a circle of friends, a network of colleagues, or a collection of far-flung individuals united by a shared identity such as race, ethnicity, sexual orientation, and so on. While it is true that we must experience some sense of kinship with members of a group in order to feel that we truly belong there, we do not need to belong to a group in order to feel a connection with any individuals within it. After all, if the intensity of our connection with any one person was predicated on shared group membership, we wouldn't experience genuine closeness with people outside these identity-based groupings.

In the modern world, tribalism (another way of referring to the communal impulse that evolution has supposedly equipped us with) does not make us feel safer, less alienated, or more content with our lives. One has only to look at our polarized politics to realize that, in fact, it does the opposite. And yet, in a world where joining and conforming are highly valued, being an otrovert is often perceived as a problem. Otroverts are frequently exhorted to "go with the flow" or "be a team player": in other words, put their true non-belonger nature to the side in order to fit into the social puzzle. Because otroverts can be quite gregarious and social when interacting one-on-one, people are often confused by their disinterest in joining group activities or reluctance to attend events where they will be forced to socialize with many people all at once.

If you fit in, others will let you be. This is why many otroverts spend their time trying to belong. Yet, for them, attempts to conform, be an insider, and experience togetherness is futile. They are not communal people and therefore cannot truly feel like a member of a group even if invited and encouraged. Nor do they want to.

And therein lies one of the greatest benefits of being an otrovert: once you accept and understand who you are, you become free from the tremendous social pressures that group membership imposes. When you have no affinity for any particular group, your sense of self-worth is not conditioned on the group's approval. You are not obligated to endorse the collective position, opinion, or point of view. You get to enjoy closeness and connection in individual relationships, while being exempt from the social contract that requires you to prioritize "the good of the group" and fulfill social needs over personal ones. You learn how to separate what you inherently know to be true from what you were indoctrinated to accept as true. And, best of all, you know no other way to think other than to think for yourself.

That's what this book is all about. It aims to describe and explain the great freedom and fulfillment that come from living life off the communal grid, while also highlighting the outsize value that the otrovert perspective contributes to the world. Although conventional wisdom is necessary for stability, revolutionary ideas are crucial to progress, so we must learn to tolerate them rather than shut them away. As Freud said, "It remains a fact, indeed, that great decisions in the realm of thought and momentous discoveries and solutions of problems are possible only to an individual working in solitude."

Over the years of my work with my patients, I've become increasingly aware of how being an otrovert myself has shaped my therapeutic philosophy and, in turn, my ability to help my patients. I value what most seem to ignore—the right we all have to define ourselves. When you discover your own self again after years of defining yourself by the group to which you believe you should belong, you get to appreciate your primacy in your own life and your duty to take care of yourself. There is nothing more freeing than to realize that since you cannot be anything other than yourself, it makes very good sense to like and value that person.

As you learn about the qualities of otroverts and their unique way of being in the world, you may realize that you are an otrovert, or that people in your life, perhaps very close ones, are otroverts.

But whether or not you recognize yourself or someone you know in these pages, I hope it will help you see how the otrovert experience can enrich the collective conventional wisdom about how to exist in the world. Whether or not you are an otrovert, your most enduring relationship is that between you and yourself. By strengthening that relationship, you can also access the mental space and energy to know and connect with others more deeply, and on your own terms.

Submitting your life to the group for review inevitably leads to the relinquishing of control over your own happiness. As philosopher Friedrich Nietzsche wrote, "Freedom is the will to be responsible for ourselves." It is my hope that this book will help you claim your inner freedom.

PART I

THE FOUNDATIONS OF NON-BELONGING

1

What Is an Otrovert?

Otrovert

[noun, adjective ot-truh-vert; verb ot-truh-vert] An "otrovert" embodies the personality trait of non-belonging: remaining an eternal outsider in a communal world. Unlike those with relational disorders, otroverts are empathetic and friendly, yet struggle to truly belong in social groups, despite no apparent behavioral distinctions from well-adjusted individuals.

"I can't explain it. He is a sweetheart. A beautiful boy inside and out, and so brilliant." This was how a session with N, a longtime patient of mine, began some years ago. Instead of talking about herself, she wanted to talk about her son, A. He was a freshman in high school, and in spite of coming from a warm, loving family with attentive parents, he'd started having social difficulties during the last year of middle school. But his issues were of a kind his mother had never really heard of or seen. He wasn't being bullied or left out or made uncomfortable by peer pressure—the usual issues at that age. In fact, she said, "he's happy going to school and gets straight As. Everyone loves him, and he gets invited to all the parties but mostly doesn't go."

He wasn't depressed or anxious and had several close friends, if not a big social group. But he turned down almost every invitation for social gatherings and trips and she couldn't understand why. "For a teenager, he's not moody or angry," she reflected. "But he is so closed off. I never know what he thinks, and he won't discuss why he doesn't want to go away to camp with his friends, who keep inviting him. The fact that he doesn't seem to care that he might be being left behind socially makes me worried the most. How can it be that at the age of fourteen, he has no interest in joining in with the other boys?"

I had seen this before. No parent likes to watch their child struggle socially—a concern that becomes even more pronounced in puberty, when being excluded has severe effects on mood, sense of well-being, and even ability to function. But N added a twist to that. She was not worried that A was unpopular. She was worried that he was somehow fundamentally different from the rest, in spite of the fact that he was an intelligent and in many ways precocious kid: "I recall when he was four, his pediatrician's nurse confessed that she found herself wanting to share her life's difficulties with him, only to catch herself at the last moment," she told me. And this nurse wasn't the only one; other adults—relatives, family friends, and even teachers—also found themselves wanting to confide in him, forgetting he was so young. "My mother is convinced he's an empath—whatever that means. But I don't want him to be special. I want him to be a regular teenager." N's voice broke as she spoke. "And not caring about your social life at this age is not normal," she said.

I agreed that his indifferent attitude to what his peers considered great fun was unusual but reassured her that it didn't sound like a psychiatric condition to me. I asked if A had a therapist and whether he'd done neuropsychological testing. Yes, to both, she said. "His testing showed high intelligence, emotional maturity, and no cognitive issues. The therapist said that he is an enigma to her, which does not give me great confidence."

Three weeks later, I sat with A in my office. He entered shyly, as would be expected from a fourteen-year-old. He was handsome, casually dressed, charming, and calm. I said, "Your mother is worried that you have no FOMO," and we both chuckled before he said earnestly, "You have FOMO when you fear missing out. But if you know you are not missing out, there is no fear." I wanted to better understand his way of seeing things and asked him to describe his experience of attending parties and other social events. "I just feel weird," he said, "like I'm not part of it, which is odd as these are all my friends. I know they like me and are happy I'm there, but I still don't feel connected. I feel lonely or bored only when I am with many people, and not when I'm with one or two close friends or when I'm alone." Then he added, clearly frustrated, "I don't like to say those things because it makes me sound like an alien. Do you think there's something wrong with me?"

I certainly didn't think anything was wrong with him, but I wondered if *he* did and asked him. "Yes," he said, echoing his mother's words. "I think I am not normal. Why don't I like whatever my friends like? It can't be that they are all wrong and only I am right."

It wasn't hard to see why he felt this way. Crossing all cultures and traditions, one force rules teenage groups: pressure to fit in. So how do we understand someone like A, who does not care about fitting in? The answer is simple: A was an otrovert.

A was very relieved by my explanation. I invited him to come and speak with me again after he had given some thought to this way of thinking about himself, and when he did, he said that our conversation had provided a flash of clarity, making him realize that a sense of not belonging was the common thread of most of his social difficulties.

He asked me to explain this to his parents, which I did, urging them not to pressure him to be "like all the other kids." At first, this was not easy on them. People around them were always insisting that they should force their son to attend parties and go to summer camp and participate in all the things that fourteen-year-old boys typically do. "He will thank you for that later," everyone insisted. "Children don't know what they need. You have to teach them." These people were wrong.

Today, to the delight of his parents, A has truly blossomed. Now twenty-four, he's getting a PhD in psychology, recently got engaged to his college girlfriend, and remains close with his best childhood friends. In some ways, he'll always remain an observer of the group and never a true participant. But he *is* a full participant in his own life: deeply satisfied with the things he chooses to do and the people he chooses to be with. This is the ideal path for an otrovert.

THE OTROVERT VIEW OF THE WORLD

In every group, there are beliefs and rules (spoken and unspoken) that members of the group must share in order to be included. Communal people—a category that includes introverts, extroverts, and outsiders who have been marginalized—want to be invited into the group, and they validate the beliefs and rules of that group by doing exactly what it prescribes. The hive mind is another name for this highly prevalent form of collective thinking

Otroverts, on the other hand, think outside the hive. They don't partake in the shared vision that group members have, and the group's center of gravity does not exert any pull on them the way it does on everyone else.

Here is a visual representation of the distinguishing factor between communal people and otroverts, and the perspective through which each views the world. Communal people look to the center of the circle, where everyone else's opinions converge. For otroverts it is the opposite. Even when they stand inside the group, they face outward.

Communal people are always oriented around the group's center, but each for a different set of reasons.

O: Otrovert
C: Communal
CO: Communal Outsiders

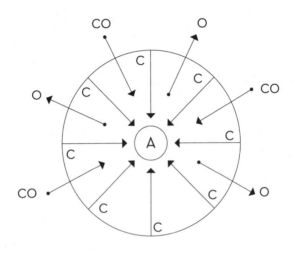

Introverts find it extremely difficult to forge deep one-on-one relationships with others and shy away from opportunities for emotional intimacy, so they seek communal relationships instead, understanding that in a circle containing many people, it is easier to keep their distance from anyone who wants to get too close. For this reason, belonging to a group—sometimes quite passionately— is important to them, even if they tend to be quiet and shy in the way they interact with it. Because social interactions quickly drain their energy, they may spend time with the group only in small doses; the shared identity and knowledge of their belonging pro- vide a sense of security and comfort.

Extroverts love an audience and participating in a shared

identity in ways that allow them to shine socially, so they need the group in order to act out those tendencies. They derive energy from being around other people and crave a degree of activity and sociability that one-on-one relationships often cannot satisfy. They thrive on the rewards of social inclusion and the high status that comes with being charismatic enough to reap them.

Outsiders are shunned by the group, often even ostracized by their peers, starting with the loosening of adult supervision in the middle school years. But because they're always yearning to be included, they are that much more oriented toward social circles that reject them.

Each of these orientations is focused on creating a shared identity that supersedes the individual one. Whether they are an introvert, an extrovert, or an outsider, the communal person is willing to sacrifice their unique but lonely journey for a common experience that offers them the impression that they are not alone.

Otroverts, by contrast, are always facing outside, even when they are standing on the inside. They are welcomed into the circle, but they never feel part of the shared experience taking place inside it. While outsiders and, to some degree, introverts are social loners, otroverts are emotional loners—they feel the most alone when surrounded by others. Many might be described as "popular loners," a contradiction the otrovert sometimes finds almost unbearable. Facing outward makes the otrovert's perspective increasingly separate from that of the collective, including other otroverts; it's as though there is an invisible yet impenetrable boundary between them and all the others. The otrovert's journey is solitary, as every human journey essentially is. The difference is that otroverts cannot ignore that truth, as most people either try or are able to do.

Each of these ways of being has its benefits and drawbacks, but regardless, none of us can choose which one we are. Much like left-handedness, being an otrovert is a cognitive feature, deeply embedded in our brain's wiring. In the same way that we now consider efforts to force left-handed children to "switch hands" (as was the common practice of parents and teachers until the early 1900s) misguided, so are attempts to "fix" otroverts by insisting that they try to fit in or belong.

Left-handed people can live comfortably in a right-handed world as long as they are left alone to be who they are; forcing them to use their right hand merely creates unnecessary discomfort and difficulty. Similarly, giving otroverts the space to be who they are will allow them to feel increasingly comfortable, especially in adulthood, when the pressure to belong lessens. Once otroverts are free from the pressures of well-meaning individuals urging them to join activities in which they have no interest, solitude becomes an opportunity for freedom, for embracing a sense of self independent of others, for allowing self-acceptance to blossom. No matter what this time alone is spent on, all that matters is that it be attuned to the needs and desires of each otrovert. This liberation from dependency on others' opinions opens up the possibility of a bespoke, self-determined life trajectory that brings contentment.

THE CORE QUALITIES OF OTROVERTS

There are many nuances to the otrovert personality, which I'll get into more in the upcoming chapters, but the following are the fundamental qualities that all otroverts share—and how they manifest in daily life.

Lack of a communal impulse.
Otroverts are not natural joiners.

- They always prefer to get together with a friend one-on-one rather than in a group. When they have to attend communal gatherings, they are the person standing off to the side, deep in conversation with another person; they never "work the room."
- They are not likely to throw themselves birthday parties and generally avoid group celebrations of any kind.
- They would rather do school projects or work assignments individually than in a group (even if that means taking on more work).
- They despise organized activities and would much rather vacation solo, even in a remote, unfamiliar destination, than go on a group trip.
- They prefer sports and activities where they can compete individually (tennis, golf, running, hiking, etc.) rather than sports where they have to play on a team (soccer, baseball, etc.).

- They have trouble being relaxed and themselves in public, no matter how common the situation. They can engage in small talk without awkwardness but are easily bored by it and find even banal interactions (like talking to a grocery store clerk or exchanging pleasantries with a neighbor) secretly irritating.
- They are uncomfortable in groups and in crowded places such as elevators or lines where small talk tends to break out to pass the time.

Otroverts are soloists who cannot play in an orchestra. They are fiercely independent, happy to sit on the sidelines, and neither need nor tolerate codependency. The writer Rudyard Kipling encapsulated this way of thinking when he wrote, "The individual has always had to struggle to keep from being overwhelmed by the tribe. If you try it, you will be lonely often and sometimes frightened. But no price is too high to pay for the privilege of owning yourself."

Always an observer, never a true participant.
Otroverts secretly feel like outsiders in any group, regardless of its members.

- They never truly feel a connection to the group itself or its shared identity, even if they connect individually with everyone in it.
- They don't like mixing people from different realms of life, even if those people know each other. For example, they

would be uncomfortable bringing a spouse to the office holiday party, where they would be responsible for integrating their spouse into the group experience.

- They don't feel an affinity with a particular sports team, an alma mater, or a company they work for. These things aren't part of their identity in the way they are for most people.

Otroverts are forever nonparticipants; they are mere observers, watching the social dance. A communal person will go on a cruise and form new bonds with strangers who become friends by the time the ship has docked again. But an otrovert will return feeling more alone than ever.

The great writer and existentialist Jean-Paul Sartre was well acquainted with this feeling, which he articulated perfectly in his first novel, *Nausea:* "I am alone in the midst of these happy, reasonable voices."

Nonconforming.
Otroverts don't just march to the beat of their own drum; they march to the beat of another instrument altogether.

- They prefer to stand out than to fit in.
- They like what they like and are not interested in popular culture. They have no interest in seeing that movie that everyone is raving about or dying to see, or dressing the way everyone else dresses (unless those things are aligned with their existing personal style or interests).

- They can be confident and charming in large gatherings when they have an assigned role or task—such as host, keynote speaker, or DJ—that visibly sets them apart from the crowd.

David Foster Wallace, another one of my favorite otrovert writers, perfectly expressed the otrovert's disdain for activities others seem to enjoy in his first novel, *The Broom of the System,* when he observed, "Modern party-dance is simply writhing to suggestive music. It is ridiculous, silly to watch and excruciatingly embarrassing to perform. It is ridiculous, and yet absolutely everyone does it, so that it is the person who does not want to do the ridiculous thing who feels out of place and uncomfortable and self-conscious... in a word, ridiculous. Right out of Kafka: the person who does not want to do the ridiculous thing is the person who is ridiculous."

Independent, original thinking.

Otroverts reject the hive mind. They don't think in the way the group collectively thinks and don't care about what the group collectively cares about. They are in touch with who they are.

- They stand by their opinions and convictions. If asked to weigh in on something at work, they aren't swayed by the opinions their colleagues have expressed.
- They do not ask for advice about how to live but readily accept advice from experts in subjects that they have no expertise in (lawyers, plumbers, etc.).

- They are specialists rather than generalists, with interests and skills that run narrow but deep. For example, when asked a question that falls outside my area of expertise, I often joke that it falls under the 80 percent of things I am bad at. But I like to think that I am not just good, but excellent, at the remaining 20 percent of things.

Virginia Woolf's *A Room of One's Own* is, of course, a seminal feminist text. But I see it also as a book that could only have been written by an otrovert who experienced daily life entirely liberated from the shared ideologies or opinions that a society tries to impose on all of its members. As she wrote in defiance, "Lock up your libraries if you like; but there is no gate, no lock, no bolt that you can set upon the freedom of my mind."

The simple reality is that there is no such thing as being "a bit otroverted." It's binary; you either are or are not an otrovert, which means either you buy into the hive mind or you don't. Belongers have many permutations, from the fanatical adherent to the disaffected, from those who are cast out to those who are crowned. Some try to be like others; some sink into solipsism. Non-belonging, in contrast, is total and immutable. But rather than view it as a burden to carry, otroverts can learn to see the many benefits and blessings that accompany this facet of who they are. It is never too late to live your life as you and nobody else.

2

How the World
Misunderstands Otroverts

Unlike many other human variations, otroversion is a cognitive style that doesn't necessarily result in a corresponding set of actions. It's also a feeling: an emotional response to being inherently alienated from the group. Otroverts are outsiders who are treated like insiders. Contrary to being shunned like other outsiders, they are always welcomed into the fold. They simply don't feel like they belong to the group and never did. But because they wear their discomfort quietly, they are often mistaken for other kinds of people who share this quality, for entirely different reasons. Here are the most common of those.

INTROVERTS

Introverts are shy and reclusive, mainly preoccupied with their inner world. Otroverts are acutely aware of other people and cannot find refuge inside themselves when surrounded by others. If anything, they are *too* attuned to the world around them.

My patient M had possessed this quality for as long as he could remember, though it had become more distracting with the passing years. He'd become burdened by the intense attention to mood and situation that he felt compelled to pay to everyone he came across, irrespective of how random and temporary they were in his life. This heightened awareness was born out of his inability to access the hive mind, which made every group an enigma, even when each individual within was transparent to him. He found every person (and not just the unusual people) interesting, even fascinating, and was constantly, if involuntarily, collecting data about the people around him. In the presence of a group, this cacophony of thoughts and observations, which must be considered to lack an "off switch," was exhausting for him, but he didn't find one-on-one interactions draining the way an introvert might.

He once described to me the way he experiences professional conferences: "When we have a cocktail hour followed by a sit-down dinner, I am super uncomfortable during the standing part and much better during the sitting part." He wondered why in the same place, with the same people, he could have such a different experience. I explained that the difference was in the number of possible interactions with different people. Sitting with people at a table limits your possible interactions to the three or four people around you, whereas at a cocktail hour you are basically exposed to everyone there; people come and go, exchange pleasantries, and move on.

Most people don't attach strongly to people they chat with briefly at a cocktail hour, so their transitions from one to the next are smooth and imperceptible. But M's deep interest in each person made those kinds of fleeting interactions almost painful. Like many otroverts, he couldn't handle the endless cycle of fast, casual attachment and detachment. Sitting at a table with others, while still uncomfortable, was immeasurably easier, but once dinner was over and people started milling around and mingling, his discomfort returned. "That's why you should leave right after the sit-down dinner," I explained. "Otroverts are masters of the 'Irish exit.'"

While some otroverts avoid this feeling by spending a lot of time alone, their emotional discomfort can present very differently in public compared with the behavior of introverts. Whereas introverts prefer to fade into the background, otroverts love the spotlight. M, for example, is not reserved or shy; he is outgoing, speaks a lot, and is entertaining. He is in his element when the group is small or when he has a social role to play that distinguishes him from the rest, and can be very confident and vocal in a small-group gathering. (I call this being a "pseudo extrovert" and will have more to say about it in chapter 4.) Because otroverts do not compare themselves to others, know what they are good at, and need no reassurance, they can come across as cocky rather than diffident or deferential, as introverts often are. They enjoy solitary time, but their solitude is not about detachment from the rest, like it is for introverts, but about a strong attachment to the self.

NONCONFORMISTS

The most passionate individualist can still belong to a group. Even if it is a "herd of individuals" in which members believe they're each unique, they are nonetheless part of a group bonded by common identity; nonconformists tend to band together, just like conformists. For otroverts, however, individualism is not a philosophical stance, or even a choice. Otroverts are individualists by default. Their nonconformism is not an act of rebellion, a means of self-expression, or a bid for attention. It is an essential trait that informs how they see their world.

Society compels humans to perceive their reality as closely as possible to the way those around them do. (Indeed, psychosis is defined as having private rather than communal perceptions.) As a result, communal people are so easily influenced by others that most can be convinced that something exists even if they don't perceive it themselves. Not only that, but they feel reaffirmed by the belief that "everyone knows" something, even if they don't poll "everyone" regularly. Once convinced that something is "the norm" (another communal tool), most people accept it without much inquiry or second thought and often never revisit the concept. Nonconformists are not immune to this; after all, they must believe that the norm exists in order to rebel against or subvert it. Otroverts, on the other hand, don't recognize the existence of the norm in the first place.

The arrival of the internet has brought better and more effective strategies to ensure conformism, one unintended consequence of the information superhighway. Beyond allowing ideas and trends to travel faster and spread more widely, the very design of the social web ensures that the communal impulse controls the dissemination of information; algorithms favor eyeballs, which means that the more people who have viewed or engaged with a news article, a social media post, or a product recommendation, the more likely others are to view and engage with it. Hence "influencers" (the epitome of communal tools), whose success is based on a circular argument: people accept what the influencer suggests because they are an influencer, and they are an influencer because many people have accepted what they suggest. On the internet, one need not be an expert—or even pretend to be one—to get others to agree with one's opinions and follow one's advice. The only factor is popularity (in the form of likes and followers), and popularity grows by consensus. For the same reasons, *any* kind of dissent fails to attract attention in the virtual landscape that the consensus efficiently and convincingly controls.

Otroverts aren't susceptible to this, or any kind of social influence. Their perceptions and preferences are influenced by their personal interests and point of view rather than by group consensus. Otroverts cannot be coerced to relinquish their version.

A rose can be a rose when everyone sees a rose. But the idea of a rose—its interpretation—can be very different for the otrovert, who cannot be coerced to relinquish their version, even if it differs from that of the majority.

Take, for example, a flag. For communal people, a flag is imbued with special value as a symbol of unity for those identifying with it. But for the otrovert it is merely a piece of cloth. An otrovert I'll call T recalls how, during her senior year in high school, as all her classmates were accepted to and enrolled in various colleges, stickers bearing the schools' names began to appear, one by one, on the bumpers of their cars. To her classmates, these bumper stickers were both an announcement of their future plans and a declaration of belonging to the college community they had agreed to join, but for T, who had also received such a sticker along with her acceptance letter, it was just a piece of paper with adhesive on one side. She wasn't trying to be different from the rest when she threw hers in the trash; she simply didn't see any point in putting it on her car. Otroverts see the same picture as all the rest. However, they don't give it a communal meaning or interpretation.

Being unbound by convention and untethered from the communal wisdom gives otroverts an exhilarating sense of freedom and autonomy. Instead of relying on the collective to mold their explanations of the world, they can shape and reshape their own explanations at will—a type of freedom many communal people find scary.

SOCIAL ANXIETY

Patient DC came to see me after having suffered from anxiety for many years. She had been diagnosed and treated for social anxiety in the past but had found no relief.

She described her condition as "outside anxious versus indoor calm." In a crowd, she felt overwhelmed, crippled by anxiety, and desperate to escape back home. Even when she was surrounded by good friends, the stress of being out in the world did not dissipate. "Strangely, they become a part of all the rest," she explained, "and I feel very lonely and lost. The harder they try to understand and help me, the worse I feel."

Good friends typically lessen social anxiety in public; their familiarity mitigates the fear of the unknown. But this was not happening for DC. Next, I asked her to be specific about situations in public or away from home where she *didn't* feel anxious. She came up with being in her car and sitting at an outdoor café or restaurant. Then she added that in a movie theater, she only felt comfortable sitting in the last row—and that the same was true on buses and trains. "I don't like people looking at me from the back, so if I sit in the back, I feel less anxious even if the bus is very crowded."

Next we moved on to her work life, which took place in a huge office building in Midtown Manhattan. When I suggested it must be very hard to work among so many people, she replied that although visiting other office buildings caused her discomfort, at her own office, she was all right. There were clearly a number of public situations in which she was *not* experiencing anxiety, so I asked her to look at those as a separate group and see if there was a common thread among them. She'd never considered it from that angle. "It has felt like one big blob of anxiety!" she told me. "But now that I think of it, I don't get why sitting outdoors, even on a busy street, is easier than sitting indoors in the same café. It's equally crowded and loud." She paused for a second. "Maybe I also have claustrophobia?" Then she smiled. "I guess I'm even weirder than I thought!"

I countered with a different possibility: the difference between those two states was her relationship to the people she shared space with. In situations that made her uneasy, like standing in line behind half a dozen others at a grocery store, she was being forced to "participate" in the crowd. But in the other situations, like sitting alone in her car or at an outdoor café, she was an observer of a group rather than an active participant in it. Even in a theater or on a crowded bus, sitting in the back seat gave her an observer's view. She needed to be able to read the room to find her place in it and feel comfortable.

In analyzing her triggering situations through the otrovert prism, it became clear why her previous treatment did not work: because it was designed for socially anxious belongers, whose discomfort is rooted in a sense of self-consciousness about their deviation from what others consider "normal" rather than a sense of non-belonging. Because otroverts aren't socially phobic, tactics to relieve them of social phobia don't help. Through our work together, DC came to understand that she did not feel self-conscious about appearing unlike others and that the solution to her anxiety was not learning to be more comfortable blending into the crowd. Non-belonging is normal for otroverts and need not be corrected. Instead of learning to belong, the otrovert's goal should be to understand their true strengths and limitations and, in doing so, develop a keen appreciation of themselves. Doing this work led DC to make choices that were better suited to her needs, which immediately liberated her from her difficulties.

MARGINALIZATION

Socially marginalized people are those who want to be part of a group but are sidelined, ejected, or never admitted into the fold to begin with. Otroverts are not cast out of the group against their will; they never belonged there in the first place.

Outwardly, otroverts can seem like part of the group, especially during the early decades of life. They can be popular, well liked, and even viewed as leaders. Based on their social position, they can appear to the observer to be successful insiders, but they always feel like outsiders. The otrovert's sense of non-belonging, in other words, does not reflect their actual social standing. Unlike unpopular insiders, they are not bullied, ostracized, or uninvited. But the dissonance between looking and acting like an insider while feeling like an outsider is tiring, leading them to withdraw from the group in favor of one-on-one relationships and avoiding unnecessary social obligations. They create a comfort zone where they are unencumbered by group dynamics, protecting their energy with self-imposed social boundaries.

NEURODIVERGENCE

Behavioral predictability is essential for social comfort among strangers. In following a predictable set of socially prescribed rules, we are constantly (if subconsciously) seeking to reassure others that we can be trusted, and they reciprocate in kind.

Neurodivergent people are divergent only relative to neurotypical people, who encounter them in ways that the collective psyche finds unpredictable. That is especially true for people on the autism spectrum, who have a number of cognitive traits that make it difficult to conform to the social scripts with which neurotypical people are comfortable. Those traits include the following:

- Difficulties in understanding social cues and engaging in typical social interactions
- Challenges in verbal and nonverbal communication
- Engaging in repetitive behaviors and having highly focused interests
- Sensory sensitivities, such as adverse reactions to specific sounds or textures

Otroverts do not display any of these cognitive particularities. Nor do they display the characteristics associated with ADHD, which is essentially an inability to manage the interplay between being attentive to the task at hand and suppressing other stimuli that may grab one's attention. People with ADHD struggle to fixate on one specific aspect of their awareness, in some cases, to the point where they can't concentrate on what a conversant is saying, are forgetful, and are constantly distracted and fidgety. Those neurocognitive symptoms are often interpreted as "bad behavior," which is why children and teenagers with ADHD are often shunned by the group. But people with ADHD are fundamentally communal people who, in the best-case scenario, are aware of their inattention and the disruption it causes and make efforts to adhere to the rules one must adhere to in order to belong.

Otroverts are neurotypical. Their brains function no differently than those of communal people, and they display no discernible behavioral differences from neurotypical people. As I've said, the experience of non-belonging is completely internal. Unlike people with ADHD, otroverts don't struggle with focus or attention—if anything, they are above average in their attentiveness. Because otroverts are very considerate and nonconfrontational and make a great effort to be predictable to others—often at great expense to themselves—they do not elicit the kinds of negative reactions that neurodivergent people often do.

Willfully not belonging in a world made for joiners can be challenging. However, it is not an impediment to any pursuit the otrovert wishes for and can even be the otrovert's greatest gift.

3

The Meek Rebel

When we think of revolutionaries—people who think outside the bounds of regular social structures—we picture strong and forceful people who overturned the prevailing order and changed the course of history. Many examples immediately spring to mind: Robespierre, Marx, Lenin, and Simon Bolívar, to name a few, along with some horrible dictators such as Hitler, Mao, and Stalin. What all these people have in common is that their rebellion invariably involved rallying other people: supporters, collaborators, and bystanders on one hand, and opponents on the other. Whether this took the form of a small, underground uprising or a swell of public sentiment, it was always a shared experience.

Otroverts think outside the bounds, too, but all their revolutionary ideas are private, contained within themselves. Otroverts are therefore what I call meek rebels. Meek rebellion is not shared, violent, or even noticeable, for the most part. But it does have a purpose for the individual; it is the non-belonger's response to living in a communal world.

Meeting a meek rebel is invariably a pleasant experience. They are naturally very polite and tend to be people pleasers: confrontation averse and often considerate to a fault. Any social discomfort that their unorthodox, counterintuitive, or countercultural ideas might cause is mitigated by a reluctance to express them. Eager to accommodate, careful not to disturb, and mortified by intrusion on others, they may be mistaken for weak or self-effacing. But this disarming attitude is far from a weakness; it is a survival tactic. Even when finding the consensus intolerable or wrongheaded, otroverts behave cautiously, well aware that questioning or protesting would disrupt social harmony. They would never, for example, attend a political rally, participate in a walkout to protest a company policy, or mingle with fans of a particular sports team while wearing the shirt of its rival (at least not of their own volition). Though they often disagree with how the captain is steering, they do not care to rock the boat.

This is in part because being themselves in the presence of the group is perilous to otroverts, as it may call attention to their variation from those surrounding them. Without the natural impulse to conform to the common denominator, they must carefully observe, learn, and practice adhering to the unspoken rules of engagement as a means of camouflaging their internal rebellion and nonconformism. The meek rebel dutifully stands in line, waits for green lights, says the appropriate thing, and so on—not instinctively, but through an inexorable process of observing how others behave for cues. But while they are often sticklers for the rules, they never respect them intellectually.

Though otroverts are not deliberately subversive, this complete freedom from conformism may elicit subversive ideas that in some cases can influence the multitudes, or even the course of history. Galileo, who helped change the way we understand the cosmos, is a prime example of this. Having realized, as a result of his experiments and observations, that the earth revolves around the sun, he faced the wrath of the Catholic Church, which allowed no challenge to the conventional thinking that the earth was the center around which everything else revolved. He quickly recanted his discovery under the threat of death, but he never stopped rebelling internally, as he knew he was right. Eventually, of course, he was proved correct.

This inner rebelliousness also extends to hive traditions such as ceremonies and holidays. Shared traditions or rituals— be they religious, national, or originating in the surrounding community—rarely feel compelling to otroverts, who struggle to anchor themselves in the social background of these traditions. Even the milestones typically deemed worthy of celebration— birthdays, anniversaries, graduations—feel arbitrary to otroverts.

Otroverts do, however, anchor themselves in personal habits and traditions. This preference for personal rituals over shared ones generally frees otroverts from unnecessary (and unpleasant) obligations like religious services, college reunions, and New Year's

Eve celebrations, but at the same time, it can also make them inflexible and rigid about their habits and routines.

The insistence on their own routines and traditions often renders otroverts unadventurous, lacking in carefree spontaneity, and apprehensive or insecure when forced out of their habitual comfort zone. The same daring spirit that takes them to the uncharted regions of thought is absent from the experiential side of life. This is entirely by choice. Freedom for otroverts is an internal experience rather than a physical one. They value their peace of mind over "excitement" and self-control over experimentation and risk-taking. Anything that might cause an adrenaline rush—metaphorically or literally—is unappealing to them, as it carries the risk of losing control. Even in the most mundane, everyday situations, losing control is a threat to their autonomy.

One patient of mine described obfuscating trivial and meaningless facts of his daily life—things like what he ate for lunch and where—as one of his favorite acts of internal rebellion. "The trivial, harmless nature of my fibbing serves as a little dig into the very people I feel alienated from," he explained, referring to these small lies as "otrovert aggressive acts." This kind of covert disobedience to the group gives otroverts an exhilarating sense of freedom. It is a way of defending their inner world—which is their life's most important dimension—without creating unwanted conflict or attracting unwanted attention.

This tendency toward outward meekness is not a problem in and of itself. However, it could become problematic for an otrovert growing up in a family that views gentleness as a weakness or even a character flaw. In those families or environments, otroverts—and particularly boys—are often forced into activities that are considered emotionally strengthening, or "character building." Sadly, while often made with good intentions, attempts to force otroverts "out of the comfort zone" frequently put them in exactly the kinds of situations that cause them emotional anguish. The more their parents and teachers and peers attempt to "fix" them so that they can be more like all the other kids, the more uncomfortable, emotionally exhausted, and defeated many otroverts become. Their meekness eventually overtakes their internal rebellion, and a form of learned helplessness sets in as their very way of being in the world, impossible for others to understand, is taken from them. This can lead some to collapse into the mental health system or simply retreat into a solitary life devoid of the rewarding connections they could have had.

In my first year of residency training, I was assigned to the case of an eighteen-year-old man who had spent most of his teenage years in the hospital's psychiatric day program, where he was diagnosed with schizophrenia. I'd been told that E was awkward and shy and found it difficult to maintain eye contact, but one-on-one with me, he was very expressive and sensitive and displayed no delusions, hallucinations, or other symptoms of psychosis, a fact that I initially attributed to the large dose of medication he was on. He also wrote poetry and was well-read and neatly groomed. None of this was consistent with the presentation of schizophrenia, which is self-neglectful, flat, and unemotive. And yet, the diagnosis of schizophrenia seemed evident to all the experienced staff members. As a rookie psychiatrist at the time, I considered my failure to elicit "schizophrenia symptoms" a matter of lack of experience or ineptitude. I assumed he must be suffering from another "type" of schizophrenia that I had yet to come across.

We met daily, as was the practice in the clinic, and soon formed a friendly rapport. We discussed science fiction and other shared interests, and E was consistently engaged, spontaneous, and bright. Speaking to his parents for more background, I found them doting, frightened, and heartbroken about their only son's dire diagnosis. All of that was understandable. Then I asked why they had first become concerned about him. They answered that while E had always been a friendly and gentle child who did relatively well in school, in recent years he had been "isolating" in ways they found concerning. He had a few friends, but he only liked to spend time with them individually for reasons unclear to his parents, and, like most teenage boys, he was awkward with girls. Though his classmates considered him a little "weird," he didn't seem to care and was happy to be in his room, building model airplanes and tinkering with radios and other electronic devices. He did not seem remotely fazed by his aloneness. E's school counselor had mentioned the possibility of autism, but he didn't exhibit the symptoms of that either. When asked to explain his problem, all he could tell the counselor was that he felt "disconnected" from others. With no other theories on the table, when doctors delivered the diagnosis of schizophrenia, his parents never questioned it.

As the weeks went by, I became even more skeptical of the schizophrenia diagnosis. At last, I decided to try tapering the antipsychotic medications while watching E closely for the emergence of psychosis. It never appeared. In fact, without the medications' side effects, E became more animated in public, and his mood brightened considerably. I was certain his diagnosis was incorrect, but I didn't know what to call his state of being—as far as I could tell, he was a friendly and gentle young man who simply needed considerable time off from his peers.

After two years, I concluded my training and left the hospital. E and I continued to communicate for years after that. He was discharged and started volunteering at a center for intellectually disabled individuals, a calling that he connected with so strongly that he proceeded to study counseling and eventually became a director of the agency. He did not take medications, nor was he ever readmitted, though he also struggled to build a rich personal life. I now believe that had I fully understood the true nature of his difficulties during our time together or even soon after, I could have offered a more productive and optimistic vision of his future, along with the assurance that being an otrovert was in no way an impediment to fulfilling it.

4

The Pseudo Extrovert

We are all familiar with extroverts: they are the people who are always the life of the party, who seem to know everyone and excel at talking to people in any situation.

Many (though not all) otroverts are what I call "pseudo extroverts." They may feel uncomfortable with a group of people, but not in the way that shy or introverted people do. They don't find themselves tongue-tied or refrain from attracting attention. In large public spaces such as on a public beach, in a packed stadium, or even on a crowded street—anywhere many strangers congregate—they are prone to discomfort and may feel awkward and inhibited. But when they are in more contained and familiar circumstances, they can be quite charming and sociable.

They don't readily engage in small talk and find it hard to hide their disinterest in popular culture. But given the chance to tell a funny story or a joke or listen empathically, otroverts are friendly and outgoing and can engage in meaningful conversation. But the boundary between self and others remains. Otroverts are solitary at heart, and the gregarious persona they adopt for public display is often a protective shield with which they fiercely guard their inner life.

Playing the gregarious socializer while being deeply private is quite taxing on otroverts, especially in the earlier stages of life. Fortunately, the pseudo-extrovert tendency usually does not linger beyond young adulthood. As otroverts get older, it becomes easier to avoid situations that make them uncomfortable. This change is eminently possible, as adulthood tends to offer opportunities for more structured socializing—an intimate dinner party or meeting one-on-one for a coffee, for example—rather than simply hanging around in big groups as we tend to do in our younger years. In contrast with the open-ended form of socializing that defines our high school and college years, most "adult" events have a purpose and often a start and end time. And in the workplace, unlike in school, there are ample opportunities to form one-on-one friendships, engage in more structured socializing (inviting a colleague to lunch, for example), and choose a career centered on individual work rather than group projects.

One otrovert recalled for me how, in her first year of college, she couldn't bear how all the students in her dormitory left their doors open all the time and were constantly wandering in and out of each other's rooms, forming and re-forming groups in the common room or out on the lawn. She was interested in forming friendships with some of her individual fellow students but had no interest in the constant shared experience, in spite of always being invited in and even urged to join. She was able to attend campus events and even parties so long as she knew about these events in advance, but the concept of "hanging out"—spontaneously and without any real structure or purpose—was foreign, confusing, and, as she put it, "frankly, quite boring" to her.

This is not uncommon for otroverts. Despite having no real desire to participate in what all the others are doing, in their adolescent and early adult years, when they are most susceptible to social pressures and to the gravitational pull of the group, otroverts *want to want* to do these things.

The social pressure to blend in can be powerful, especially during those teenage and young adult years. But there is an exception to this: when otroverts are handed a social role—such as team leader, host, coach, or presenter, for example—they often shine, even in large groups. It may seem like a narcissistic need to be regarded as someone special, but a designated position makes group attendance tolerable by giving otroverts a socially acceptable way to maintain their boundaries and set themselves apart. It does not have to be an elevated role, only a very different one from the rest. For example, one teenager I know feels compelled to attend his friends' parties, as he doesn't want to be rude, but he always plays the role of DJ so he doesn't blend in with the crowd.

This brings me back to my patient DC, whom you met in chapter 2—the "outside anxious versus indoor calm" otrovert who was most comfortable in the world as an observer. My discovery of this trait led me to ask her if she had trouble with public speaking, a role that focuses the spotlight on an individual—the exact opposite of being an observer—which is often difficult even for non-otroverts.

"Not at all!" she declared, happy to find that a situation many find hard was actually anxiety free for her. "I like to make presentations, and I have no stage fright." When I asked her what she tended to do after she finished speaking, I got a typical otrovert answer: "I usually make a beeline to the bathroom and sneak back to my room. I can't stand cocktail conversations." But the public speaking itself, notorious for causing performance anxiety among all personality styles, was no problem for her at all. This is because standing alone at the podium or being onstage at an event is an assigned social role that differentiates the otrovert from everyone else in the room.

I experienced this myself when, at age fourteen, I started to volunteer in a hospital. It was a humble position—I was assigned to roll a small confectionary cart from room to room selling candies to bedridden patients and handing out newspapers and small toiletries. It was very satisfying, as the patients looked forward to the cart's arrival—and mine, since I was its lucky driver. But the real bonus of this volunteer work was that I got to wear a white coat, which allowed me to imagine that some people might think I was an unusually young doctor—some kind of prodigy who had managed to complete medical school before he was old enough drive a car (in retrospect I'm sure nobody thought this, but at fourteen my imagination was unlimited). The only thing that shattered the fantasy was the word "volunteer" embroidered on the breast pocket of the coat. I did everything to hide this scarlet letter so that I could play my role to the maximum. I fashioned an awkward Woody Allen–esque way of keeping my hand on my pocket in order to obscure the evidence that I was just one of many young volunteers racking up community service hours. I must have been quite a sight: a tall and skinny redhead with horn-rimmed glasses walking everywhere while holding his hand over his heart. But I discovered that standing out in this way made me feel good and confident. It created a clear boundary between me and them, which made my experience more manageable.

That said, the role need not be obvious to create inner calm; it can be an "undercover" role, such as a medical professional visiting a different hospital or a professor on the grounds of a different university: anything that affirms the otrovert's sense that they are different from those around them. That knowledge of their difference aligns their outer experience with their inner one and feels harmonious in a way that masquerading as an extrovert does not.

In looking back on their pseudo-extroverted years, adult otroverts often find it hard to reconcile their past performance with their present reticence. From the moment they are freed from the need to perform, the otrovert's authentic self finally has space to emerge, which brings them the peace of mind they need.

Recall that this was very much the case for my patient A, whose story was the first I told you in chapter 1. Once he was in his twenties, the point at which it becomes easier for otroverts to be less conspicuous about not joining, he was able to settle into a very happy life, full of work and relationships that he chose on his own terms and that brought him real connection and joy.

5

The Creative

Creativity is the act of making something that has not existed before. It is often said that the greatest innovations—in art, science, or any other creative field—are collaborations: the products of many gifted minds working together. Although it is true that it often takes a village to advance cutting-edge knowledge, execute an innovative solution, or bring a new idea to fruition, true creativity always starts with some kind of breakthrough insight, idea, or revelation that tends to be the product of a single mind. As novelist John Steinbeck noted, "Our species is the only creative species, and it has only one creative instrument, the individual mind and spirit of man."

Once the miracle of creation has taken place, the group can expand, extend, and apply it, but the collective never invents anything. Whether in music, art, poetry, mathematics, or philosophy, "the preciousness," as Steinbeck puts it, "lies in the lonely mind of a man." Think of Galileo, van Gogh, Mozart, or Plato, not to mention Pythagoras, Euclid, Newton, Maxwell, Einstein, and Bohr. Each of them broke with reigning conventions to illuminate a different view of nature, art, or philosophy that left a mark on the world. And while they were eventually joined by many others who adopted or built on their ideas, those ideas were (at least initially) theirs and theirs alone.

It isn't easy to conjure up an idea that is not derived from past conventions, and there is no formula for coming up with revolutionary discoveries. But, while we cannot codify a distinct process for thinking, hearing, or seeing something as never before, we can probably make one assumption: it requires being unencumbered by limits that communal thinking places on the individual mind. Because this kind of independent thinking comes naturally to otroverts, many are deeply creative.

The difference between a true creative and someone who is merely gifted, artistic, or even exceptional is that the former does not aim to be the best at something; they do something no other has ever thought to try. Astrophysicist Neil deGrasse Tyson has made this his "personal philosophy in life," saying, "If somebody else can do something that I am doing, they should do it. And what I want to do is find things that would represent a unique contribution to the world—the contribution that only I, and my portfolio of talents, can make happen. Those are my priorities in life."

Otroverts are able to make unique contributions for two reasons. First of all, they are not susceptible to the collective notions about what makes a work of art, literature, music, or any other creative endeavor "good." This is not because the otroverts live as hermits, without exposure to these outside influences, but rather because they are impervious to the opinions of others, past or present, when it comes to creative decisions. They don't need to tune out the white noise of those alternate perspectives because they rarely register these perspectives in the first place, and even when they do, they simply don't feel the urge to use them as a means of comparison. The result is that just the basic act of thinking can lead the otrovert to creative discoveries that unintentionally subvert the communal wisdom.

Second, otroverts have no need for others' approval or agreement. When you are not trying to convince others of your work's merit, and when you have no fear of judgment or criticism, that is when you get to truly create, without inhibition.

The painter Frida Kahlo once said, "I don't give a shit what the world thinks. I was born a bitch, I was born a painter, I was born fucked. But I was happy in my way. You did not understand what I am. I am love. I am pleasure, I am essence, I am an idiot, I am an alcoholic, I am tenacious. I am; simply I am." Kahlo, a true otrovert, was far from reclusive and loved to hang around with the rich and famous (before becoming bedridden after a terrible trolley accident). But there existed within her a deep inner well of inspiration that was impenetrable to outside influences, including the pressure to make her self-portraits less "masculine"; her silent rebellion against these influences was what inspired the exaggerated mono-brow and faint mustache that became the signature of her self-portraits. "I never paint dreams or nightmares," she wrote. "I paint my own reality...and I paint whatever passes through my head without any other consideration."

Being free of the "communal wisdom," otroverts do not concern themselves with what is achieved through the act of creation; it does not have to be essential so long as it introduces something original and not derivative. It does not even have to be pleasing so long as it is unprecedented. Because otroverts are always facing in a different direction, they are able to access new perspectives to illuminate what is hidden.

6

The Empath

We all know the exhortation to "put yourself in someone else's shoes." It's a way of encouraging empathy for a friend, a colleague, a family member, or even a stranger going through something difficult. It is also a natural extension of the collective's bias toward sameness. It assumes that once you can get into those other shoes, you'll understand how that person feels because we all feel the same thing in similar circumstances. One of the rewards of communal life is the feeling that we can understand one another through empathy. The communal person trusts that we all love the same way, hate the same way, fear the same things, and feel the same things. This is literally second nature in humans to the point where it is the basis for one of the tenets of communal morality: Do unto others as you would be done to.

The power of this statement, of course, relies on the assumption that we all want to be treated in the same way. The notion that we all have the same needs and desires is so ingrained that we never think to stop and consider periodically whether it's really true. But when we assume everyone is the same, we cannot access a deeper level of empathy because we lose the ability to imagine what another person is going through.

That level of empathy, which is very hard for communal people to exercise, comes quite naturally to otroverts. They never imagine what they would do in your shoes. Instead, they imagine what *you* would do; they look at your circumstances the way *you yourself* see them. The ability to distinguish another's perspective from their own also explains why otroverts tend to be radically nonjudgmental. So often, a failure of empathy is the result of someone looking at a person's choices or actions and thinking, "Had I been in that situation, I would have handled it better." Judgment, which is really inserting your own beliefs and values between you and the other person, precludes the possibility of truly seeing things through their eyes. The otrovert's ability to respond to a person's inner reality without judgment or bias creates a high level of empathetic insight.

When communal people find themselves in a group, they automatically experience what I call "the Bluetooth phenomenon"— the ability to send signals to and pick up signals from anyone within a certain perimeter. Much like a Bluetooth device, the majority of humans automatically search for connection, pairing with others when possible. Think about all those strangers in airports, in grocery stores, on city streets, who have little trouble being together. At least under normal, routine circumstances, no one consciously worries about anyone else in these situations. Yet everyone operates according to the synchronized ballet that kicks in to create social harmony when people are together, whether they are strangers or not.

The Bluetooth phenomenon is what dictates this choreography, forging a passive connection between individual minds and the local collective experience. Everyone has a role relative to all the rest. New people are joining, and others are leaving: that the minds are connected by the same Bluetooth signal makes for smooth social intermingling. It's how we know that we are expected to smile and say hello to the neighbor we encounter in the elevator, or move our shopping cart to the side of the aisle so another shopper can get by despite our general inattention to every person passing in front of our eyes: a normal response when we are among a crowd.

The Bluetooth phenomenon also mitigates feelings of aloneness, overriding the binary notions of "separate" and "together." It tells us when others around us are excited, or nervous, or fearful; it helps us read the vibes. (A notable exception to this rule is groups of teenagers, whose sense of alienation from people older than them causes disinterest and even hostility; as a result, they can't pick up a signal from the adults around them, and vice versa.)

Otroverts, of course, are unable to forge this kind of passive connection with the surrounding collective. The Bluetooth phenomenon is what allows communal people to access the minds of other people without much effort. The notion of feeling alone, as opposed to being alone, is dependent not on the presence of other humans but on our ability to access them (this is why you consider yourself alone when your neighbor is on the other side of a wall—there is no easy access). But otroverts are not wired for group affinity in the same way. That the otrovert lacks access to the Bluetooth signal makes proximity to a collective of strangers an overwhelmingly lonely experience. And the larger the group, the lonelier they feel.

Without direct access to the "cacophony of minds" that communal people are able to tap into, otroverts are compelled to compensate by paying attention to every person in sight, regardless how impersonal, fleeting, or anonymous the encounter is. Fortunately for otroverts, that granular level of attention to each individual around them is a great asset in one-on-one encounters. This is where the "bespoke" empathy they embody comes from.

When I was a child, I thought that everyone could "read other people's minds" in the way I did. I would walk to school, making mental notes about everyone I encountered—my understanding of their lives, moods, and situations, all of which I filed away in the archives of my brain. I didn't do it out of interest or fascination with any particular individual—it was simply my instinctive reaction to encountering another person. I gained nothing from it and am not even sure that most of what I conjured up was true, as there was obviously no way to verify my assumptions. But it was not voluntary; I could not turn it off.

Eventually, I discovered that while "reading" random people on the street is burdensome and futile, it was also what allowed me to forge meaningful connections in one-on-one encounters with people, no matter how brief. My teenage volunteer job at the hospital, which I mentioned in chapter 4, marked the first time I realized this. It was the first chance I had to communicate with adults on a deeper level. Some patients would strike up a conversation with me, and they were so happy to have someone to talk to that I would often return to them to continue the conversation after I had finished dispensing the candies and papers and toiletries. They told me I helped them feel less lonely, which not only made me feel wonderful but let me understand, for the first time, the power of looking at the world through someone else's eyes, of refraining from judgment, and operating from a place of pure empathy.

This was the beginning of my lifelong love affair with medicine. I was a freshman in high school with "volunteer" embroidered on my coat and no idea what illnesses the patients had or what treatment they were getting, but I felt like I was a doctor because I was helping people feel better, even if only for a few moments. That idea of what it means to be a physician has not changed throughout my years of "real" work as a doctor, helping people walk out of my office feeling better than they had when they walked in to see me.

PART II

A WORLD MADE
FOR JOINERS

7

We Are All Born Otroverts

Any attempts to understand human behavior invariably stumble over the nature/nurture dilemma, namely, which aspects of a particular behavior are innate and which are learned? We frequently encounter that duality in our daily lives: If I am easily upset, was I born hypervolatile, or has my life experience made me more sensitive to specific triggers? Am I sad because of my circumstances, or do I have an innate tendency for depression? Why do I behave this way? Is it me, or is it something I learned? Our choices and experiences can be both *hardwired* (nature) and *acquired* (nurture), to varying degrees. We consider what is hardwired to be immutable and what is acquired to be potentially modifiable, even if quite ingrained.

Our communal society has instilled the belief that each of us arrives in the world with an innate urge to belong. We are told that this is in part because, since the dawn of our species, human communities have been stitched together by the belonging impulse. Without it, the cooperation-driven advantage would not have been possible. Humans, it has long been believed, are hardwired for belonging because for our prehistoric ancestors, membership in a group or tribe increased an individual's chances of survival.

While there is merit to this theory, it is only one part of a more nuanced and complex story.

The truth is that we all arrive in the world alone and leave the world alone. Unlike many communal animals, human newborns remain helpless for so long that failing to connect with or attach to a caregiver greatly decreases their chances of survival. However, most scientific considerations of the attachment impulse conflate it with the desire to belong. And while that initial impulse to attach is innate—evolution's way of ensuring our affinity to parents and other important providers—anything beyond it must be taught.

Children do not naturally understand or feel attachment to a group of strangers at a young age. As infants, we don't know anything about our circumstances, notions of space and time, or what is happening around us. Without language, we are disconnected from the information available to the verbal human, and we lack a frame of reference to organize and differentiate between our internal and external worlds. There is no clear demarcation between the self and the other. Babies don't know anything about the relationships among the adults surrounding them, and they certainly know nothing about the many complex concepts that govern social life. In other words, they don't exhibit any recognition of a group or their place within it.

But each infant does know themself. Children are born knowing how to care for themselves by crying and fussing when they need something; however, at this young age their notions of social behavior are rudimentary, and they communicate basic needs vaguely and inefficiently.

The first two years of life are spent in this solipsistic manner, where gratifications cannot be postponed, regardless of others' needs; an infant does not understand, or care, if their mother is busy on a Zoom call at the time they demand a feeding. Then, at about age three, as the acquisition of language starts to inform their understanding of the needs and opinions of others, small children are taught to abandon the self-absorbed aspects of their behavior.

Up to this point, need gratification was provided on an unconditional basis. But now, the child begins to learn that the approval of their caregivers may be contingent on the social appropriateness of their behavior.

Socially harmonious concepts, such as "share," "wait your turn," and "let the others speak," are drilled into children, with no explanation as to why the child should prefer the group's needs over their own. We say, "This is how you make friends; this is the right way...," and we reward children for communal behavior with smiles of encouragement, hugs, high fives, and various other forms of praise. Meanwhile, at the urging of caregivers, the parallel play that characterizes toddlerhood—when children in the same space are happily occupied with different things, oblivious to their peers—is gradually replaced by more interactive forms of play that require responding to others' reactions and actions. No other cognitive behavioral conditioning occurs on this universal a scale.

This well-intentioned training shapes the entire upbringing of most children. They are taught to favor the needs of the group over their impulses and come to understand the limits of their own importance relative to that of others. The growing awareness that they are no longer the center of the universe is hard for the young child to accept, but the rewards for being social compensate. Thus, the once self-centered toddler is railroaded into a life of communality.

Most children absorb this social conditioning quite easily, albeit with the occasional bumps along the way. True otroverts are the exception. Even at a young age, they simply cannot subjugate their inner world for the sake of a shared experience, despite the exhortations of caregivers, teachers, and parents. The progression from unique individual to social animal does not unfold smoothly for them. Instead, it is met with the kind of misunderstanding and disapproval that tends to be levied toward anyone who does not toe the social line. This was certainly my experience.

In the 1960s, it was customary for Isreali children to join the Scouts once they reached fifth grade. In many ways, this organization mimicked the American version; you met with your peer group twice a week, wore the ubiquitous Boy Scout uniform, and were instructed by the teenage team leaders on doing good deeds and sacrificing your needs for the larger good. Unlike today, at the time I was joining, it was considered the "coolest" thing to do, and anyone who did not join was looked upon as "lame" and nerdy.

My parents bought me the Scout uniform with the matching scarf and leather loop to fasten it around the collar. I still remember feeling special and grown-up as I wore the uniform to the local Scout chapter. My friends and I could barely contain our excitement as we made this ritual passage from a carefree childhood to what felt at the time like our first taste of adult responsibility. We all formed a circle, sitting cross-legged on the ground as the group leader—sixteen years old—sat on a small stool and addressed us very seriously. When he finished talking about what it meant to be a junior Scout, he told us to stand at attention as he recited the pledge, and we repeated solemnly after him. It went something like this:

Be always ready.
Be ready to fulfill your duty.
Be faithful to your country and nation.
Always help others selflessly.
Always keep your sacred vow.

As I said the words out loud, I knew for the first time that I was different. While the other kids seemed awed by the duty being bestowed upon them, I felt only resistance. No matter how much I tried, I could not share their enthusiasm. Even though most of the other boys were my good friends, they suddenly appeared foreign and far away. For the first time, I felt deeply lonely; it was as if I were observing this ritual from a distance, rather than participating in it.

That night, I told my mother I didn't want to continue with the Scouts. She told me to give it another chance, so I went to two more meetings before dropping out, never to return. During the summers, all my friends would go to the wilderness to learn survival techniques and bond and have fun without the adults interfering. I lived a block away from where the buses picked them up very early in the morning and could hear the kids' excited voices ring through the air as they embarked. I envied them for being so carefree and always covered my head with my pillow to drown out their voices. I knew from experience that the instant they left, the brief FOMO would dissipate into the great relief of staying behind, but it was still painful in the moment.

I remember once my mother came into my room as I was lying in bed with the pillow over my head. She could not understand why I envied the kids for doing something I could have done myself, something I and I alone had *chosen* not to do. "Who is stopping you from going on the trip?" she asked. I could never figure out how to explain how I felt, and my mother could not understand why I couldn't be like all the other kids.

I could never explain to her why I couldn't be "normal" because I didn't know myself. I didn't understand why going on the kind of trip that most children only dream of—being left unsupervised with a group of peers to stay up late, pull pranks, and be rowdy—seemed so unbearable to me; I just knew I wouldn't be able to enjoy it the way most others did.

Today I understand why my mother was so concerned. She wanted me to partake in communal activities because she—like the parents of my otrovert patients—felt anxious about my dis-interest in what she considered "socialization." She saw that I loved school and was very friendly and outgoing when I was in my com-fort zone. But she worried about my inability to make my way in communities, since to her, and to most people, success in life is dependent on belonging. Eventually, she saw how collective activ-ities left me drained and unhappy. She did not understand me, but she loved me and wanted me to be happy. And so, thankfully, she let me be the otrovert I was born to be.

8

A Culture That Rewards Joining

We live in a culture that puts a premium on joining. Evidence of this priority begins very early in life, when we are taught to share, play nicely with other children, and align our behavior with the behavior of those around us. When others form a line, we are directed to stand in it. When others are talking quietly, we are told to lower our voices. When others play on the jungle gym, we are encouraged to get out of the sandbox and onto the monkey bars. Long before we are able to understand the codes of interpersonal behavior fully, we are taught to want to belong and are motivated to quickly conform to the expectations that communal life requires.

Meanwhile, we are presented with endless opportunities to forge affiliations with our peers: carpools, summer camps, team sports, after-school clubs, and so forth. Classrooms are often segmented into teams or cohorts, each assigned labels to reinforce group identity and belonging (e.g., red and blue teams). The ability to assimilate into these groups is seen as a prerequisite for healthy social and emotional development, and opting out is rarely an option.

The motivation to "fit in" ramps up in early adolescence, which is when we discover (often the hard way) that disregard for the group leads to unhappiness and rejection, whereas conformity confers social rewards. The desire for popularity and social approval becomes all-encompassing, just as the criteria for inclusion into peer groups become stricter and popular cliques close ranks.

This "guided joining" tapers off after age twenty or so, when groups created for us by adults (classes, after-school programs, camp, family, etc.) begin to lose externally imposed structure. With time, our growing capacity for abstract thinking allows us to join notional groups based on shared concepts and ideas, like political parties, religions, or other ideologies. This leap is the final step into full-fledged belonging.

By this point, we have learned the unambiguous lesson that in adulthood, you cannot expect groups to form organically, the way they did in your high school homeroom or your college dormitory. Instead, you have to identify potential groups and make an effort to join them, or even take part in their creation.

Similarly, the social ranking system changes. In childhood and adolescence, the group unofficially (and unfairly) assigns a particular social ranking to each one of the members based on the same attributes that govern all mammals' rankings: looks, health, and size. Those mechanisms change in adulthood. Good looks continue to be an asset, but the social ranking of adults is also based on intangible status markers such as money, class, nationality, and other nebulous "qualities." Exclusivity also plays a role: the harder the admission to the group—such as country clubs or alumni associations of elite universities—the more desirable it becomes.

Most communal people spend an inordinate amount of time on "friendship maintenance," gaining admission to and keeping up with the myriad groups they are a part of, spending time, money, and effort to be accepted, even where they are unwanted, and to "remain relevant" in the way they've always been taught matters.

On one hand, this evolution makes joining more difficult and requires a higher motivation level than ready-made childhood groups. On the other hand, it makes rejection harder to swallow. Communal people who are socially unsuccessful develop anxiety, self-esteem issues, and other mental health challenges because they have learned to equate their popularity with their sense of self.

As social life becomes increasingly self-scripted, the need to belong becomes more urgent. For many communal individuals, belonging to a group—whether it's the formal variety, like a religious congregation, or informal, like a circle of friends—provides the social support needed to ward off discomfort with the futility of life we all encounter at moments in adulthood, along with the growing awareness of the loneliness of death.

For a society, communality can be especially valuable in the face of shared hardship, when any group tends to close ranks in grim determination. A calamity like a natural disaster, war, or terror is a threat to collective safety, and its arrival means individuals are often willing to make great sacrifices, and sometimes even risk their own lives, in order to save others, including strangers. This level of altruism is rare in everyday life, because the majority of the time, getting along does not necessitate great sacrifice. Greed, inequality, competition—all things that the collective tolerates and even venerates in times of plenty—become unsustainable in times of crisis. Instead, helping others and sharing burdens rather than focusing on oneself suddenly become admirable and even heroic, bringing the social rewards that financial success and elite status bring in regular times. The higher the existential threat to the group, the greater the feeling of unity, as well as the level of sacrifice, as the group calls upon each member to do their part for the collective survival.

The COVID pandemic demonstrated this principle many times over. When it arrived, self-imposed restrictions of an unprecedented nature sprang up overnight. Businesses shut their doors, schools sent children home, and whole countries went into voluntary quarantine in an attempt to stop the spread of the virus. People kept six feet of distance from one another, stopped meeting in indoor spaces, and wore masks in public: both to protect themselves and out of consideration for others. Meanwhile, charitable donations and other forms of assistance such as food delivery to the elderly and homebound and telephone helplines serving the socially isolated increased dramatically, demonstrating the collective to indeed be stronger than the sum of its parts.

All of which reinforces the one central, immutable cultural principle in any society at any time in history: *Togetherness is preferable to aloneness.* And while this is true for many people, particularly during difficult times, it is not true for otroverts, who never feel true unity with the groups to which they are assigned even while banding together with others to ensure the members' mutual survival.

Our culture puts so much stock in communality that a different stance—the otrovert stance—is understood as pathology. If we all agree there is only one right way to move through the world, the otroverts' can only be the wrong way. Fortunately, the vast majority of people would disagree with that statement. We do not expect all people to be the same. In fact, we accept a wide variety of personalities and temperaments—and often enjoy them. Non-belonging is merely another facet of one's personality that shapes certain experiences of being human. And yet we treat it very differently from other preferences by continuing to insist that otroverts give up their true self in favor of the collective (perhaps because so many of us did undergo the forced abandonment of our own innate solipsism in exchange for social acceptance).

The pressure put on otroverts to conform is often exhausting and frustrating to both sides, but there is one thing it never is: effective. Indeed, I have many patients who come to me as adults still wondering why they can't make peace with the pressure their families and society at large put on them to go along with the expected norms.

My patient T was one such case. When we first started meeting virtually, she was emotionally paralyzed, besieged by intense anxiety that made everything feel impossible. She was on numerous psychiatric drugs, to no avail, and had been bedridden for two years. When she Zoomed with me from bed, appearing disheveled and distraught, she shook with emotion. She told me that she had always been her family's "black sheep" because she could never do anything right. She came from a very wealthy, snobbish family made up of dutiful people who had all followed the same social rules for generations. Within the family, there were unambiguous rules about how a person should conduct their life: be reserved and never showy; have good manners; have the right kind of weekend house in the right place; and, if you were a man, work in one of a small number of approved professions. Women were to focus on lunching, which was taken as seriously as though it were a profession.

T was the antithesis of all of this. From an early age, she had felt meek, diffident, and uncomfortable in her skin. She felt like her life was one long, inexorable exam, which she failed repeatedly. She understood that there was a certain "correct" way to live: a code to life that was known to others but that she simply couldn't figure out. She further thought that everyone around her, having cracked the code, was able to move easily and unerringly through life while she was always at risk of making mistakes. Her family's rigidity about what was deemed appropriate behavior made her feel that her mere presence interfered with the others' sense of harmony. Worse, she had grown to internalize the others' disapproval of her difficulties. She considered herself lazy and indulgent, self-absorbed and entitled, echoing all the criticism directed at her refusal to engage in the pageantry of communal life.

Over the years, T had been diagnosed with the entire gamut of mood and personality disorders. She'd been prescribed medications, magnetic stimulation of the brain, special diets, behavioral treatment, dialectical behavior therapy—a huge assortment of treatments that had only one thing in common: they did not work. She was sent to rehab programs—despite the fact that she did not drink alcohol and never did drugs. She adhered dutifully to every treatment suggestion, no matter how far-fetched, as she wanted desperately to feel better. But in a way, this only contributed to her misery, as her lack of progress was blamed entirely on her: "She is not trying enough" and "She does not want to get better." All of which only amplified her anxiety and left her with an increasing sense of being misaligned with the world around her, making it very hard to function.

She doubted every thought or feeling she had and was paralyzed by fear of certain failure. She'd tried to have a career, earning an MBA and a job in real estate investment, but felt profoundly disconnected from the groups of students and colleagues she encountered. Eventually, she left that position and started isolating herself for longer stretches. At a certain point, even meeting a neighbor in the hallway became too much for her. She retreated into her apartment and, other than therapy—of which she'd had a lot—had little contact with the outside world. Her doctors concluded that she was "afraid of life." Sadly, the last assumption was actually the first accurate one. But since it came at the end of long therapeutic efforts, it was stated as a verdict rather than a diagnosis—an admission of failure in treating her rather than a direction for future treatment.

But she never lost the motivation to find a way through. I'd been recommended as a psychiatrist who could help people considered resistant to treatment, and at first, she believed in me just as she had believed in every doctor who came before me, which is to say, not very much. She knew that at the deepest level, none of them truly understood her, but she also couldn't help but chastise herself for being misunderstood. She told me, "I am not good at anything. I am a freak." To which I replied, "You are very good at one thing—namely, staying in bed." Her response? "Doctor, reverse psychology has been tried plenty. It does not work on me: my entire psychology is already reversed."

I told her that I meant it seriously. She'd been telling herself she could not do anything, but she was actually very good at staying in bed. It was not good for her, but she was undeniably committed to it. Most people cannot stay in bed for long, uninterrupted periods. "It's helpful," I explained, "to find at least one thing that you are good at or at least consistent in. Staying in bed is your superpower."

She thought about it, and a little smile crept onto her face before she said, "I am a staying-in-bed specialist...the best!"

"Yes," I said. "You've perfected it into an art form."

This was the first small step in what eventually became a new life for T. Over many months and many conversations, she started realizing that staying in bed to avoid life had not succeeded in easing her suffering. This opened her up to the notion that her sense of non-belonging was actually *the cause* rather than *the outcome* of her lifelong struggles and that she would never be at peace until she learned to understand and accept this aspect of who she was. At one point, I asked her if she could think of an environment (other than her bed) that made her happy. She replied that the best time of her life was when she had traveled alone to the South Pacific islands and spent her days scuba diving and swimming in the sea.

When I suggested that perhaps it was not the best choice to continue living "landlocked" in the northeast of the country, she insisted that her misery was within her and therefore followed her everywhere. No matter where she went, she claimed, she could never break free from the idea that everyone around her was judging and criticizing her. I disagreed.

All otroverts have an internal rebellious streak—a kind of shield against indoctrination—which allows them to live as their true selves even in the face of societal pressure. But for those like T, whose rebellious streak had been crushed by a strict, uncompromising family, the inability to be indoctrinated makes life even more difficult. It is akin to the experience of someone born into a very religious family and community who secretly cannot believe in a god. No matter how hard they try, it does not happen. They can pray and go through the religious motions, but inside they feel like frauds. T thought that being an outsider despite having no perceivable "social faults" had to be the product of some personal failing that she needed to find a way to overcome. To her family, her decision not to get married or have children and her desire to live on a South Pacific island seemed capricious, impulsive, or just evidence of her willful resistance to the notion of living the life they expected. She had become convinced that she was too damaged to ever be able to master the rules of social engagement, which eventually grew so overwhelming that she dropped out altogether.

We spent the next year or so considering the possibility that even though a group of people—in this case, her family—agrees on a certain way of being and behaving, it isn't necessarily the only way. She came to understand that whatever her close circle might have expected of her, she was in no way compelled to comply— that she was allowed to have her own point of view even if the rest saw things differently, and that her otherness was neither a mental disorder not a moral failing: it was simply part of her natural wiring.

Otroverts like T find many basic tenets of communal life difficult and even baffling. These may include the commonly held notion that celebrations must necessarily involve gathering many people together in public, that the majority is usually right, that teamwork is important for progress, that it's more important to be popular than it is to be authentic, and that long-held, shared beliefs and traditions about the "right" way to behave and move through life are universally valuable.

This chronic tension between what the world believes and what the otrovert knows to be true is part of the reason why otroverts tend to present with a complex of seemingly unrelated difficulties—in T's case, isolation, depression, and lack of motivation to engage in life, along with a host of nonspecific somatic complaints including nausea, back pain, and intermittently severe abdominal cramps. Since none of these could be explained by any objective finding, she was instead diagnosed with a somatic disorder—meaning she was also (according to her doctors) inventing physical ailments. Indeed, the sum of her symptoms presented an irresistible temptation for her clinicians to label her suffering a psychiatric disorder.

Her doctor had concluded that she was "afraid of life," yet had any of them taken the time to explore the nature of those fears, they would have discovered that what T was actually afraid of was *communal* life. In particular, she feared being made to feel like there was something wrong with her every time she diverged from the rules about what was deemed socially acceptable.

To be clear, the fact that one is an otrovert does not necessarily mean that one isn't also suffering from a psychiatric disorder or experiencing some other mental health challenge. But in the vast majority of cases, the sense of non-belonging is the common thread in all their difficulties. Once otroversion is identified, everything rapidly becomes clear. Indeed, once we determined that T was an otrovert, we shifted to a new approach. The main focus of all past efforts had been getting her to be a normative member of the community, a common if misguided goal when working with otroverts. In fact, most psychological treatments for a wide range of problems aim to increase personal comfort with oneself and one's environment. In communal people, these two objectives are usually harmonious, and even synergistic: feeling more comfortable with themself helps the communal person feel more comfortable in their environment, and vice versa. In otroverts, however, the two spheres are often unsynchronized; the more comfortable an otrovert is with their inner self, the less comfortable they are in their social environment. Because the otrovert will never feel truly comfortable in a social world designed for joiners, the goal is to address their personal emotional comfort rather than try to "socialize" them.

When I suggested that T take a trip to an island with the right color of sand and water, her old fear, expressed to me a year earlier, reared its head again. "I will only prove to myself that I am unhappy everywhere I go," she said. I was also concerned about that possibility, but I knew she needed to do something to break the paralysis she was currently experiencing, and where better than a place and a setting where she already knew she felt comfortable? She was no longer on speaking terms with her family by that point, so there was no collective from which she had to fear judgment, and no pressure to justify her plan. In that sense, she was free to do as she chose in a way many people are not.

The decision was made. As so often happens in psychiatric treatment, most of the work had already happened beforehand, in T's unconscious mind. This allowed her to go from lying in bed one day to getting on a plane to the Caribbean (closer than the South Pacific, with the same calming effect) the next. The moment for action had arrived, and she had taken it. She rented a place for a month and ended up staying six. Then T came back to the United States, sold her apartment, and moved to that island.

Obviously, I present here the nutshell version of the treatment. The longer version is more complicated, and fraught with ups and downs, all of which led to her eventual realization that while no one among her family or friends approved of her finding her calling as a diving instructor on a Caribbean island, that didn't make her choice invalid. She discovered a life that could make her happy, and that was enough.

Otroverts share likes and dislikes with all people—some like the beach and some like the mountains, so to speak. It's in the realm of communal likes and dislikes where the divergence can be vast, as T experienced. Being unable to join (or genuinely partake in) what others visibly enjoy makes someone like T question their judgment, which can trigger overwhelming self-doubt or even paralysis, as it did for her. In a society governed by a set of collective rules and norms dictating the "right" way to live, it can be very hard to entertain the idea that perhaps you and the group are both "right." Of course, there is no one way to live and act and be, and the otrovert way is just another way, rather than the wrong way.

For an otrovert, accepting what we think of as the clichéd statement "It's okay to be you" is actually a monumental shift. So many of us otroverts have, like T, lived our whole lives with the experience of being misunderstood, and often judged by the group. When otroverts finally reach a place of understanding that there is nothing wrong with who they are, it is cathartic in a truly profound way.

With the realization that you don't need to force yourself to be someone you are not in order to be happy, otroverts can give themselves permission to opt out of things that cause discomfort and, in doing so, allow their authentic selves to thrive. They learn to connect even more powerfully with individuals, enjoying even deeper and more loving relationships with people they feel close to. They learn that while the world may be primarily designed for joiners, joining isn't actually mandatory for happiness.

9

The Fallacy of Fitting In

Think of a very simple creature, an amoeba, for example. It lives in the same world as we do but has a different experience. Devoid of any specialized sensory structures or brain, this unicellular organism lives a very simple life. It has no relationship or kinship to any other creature. It has no fear of the future or memories of the past. It just exists, and after a while, it either dies or is divided into two new amoebas. Even nonhuman primates, which have large brains and live in complex societies, understand their social worlds through unconscious, instinctive means. Though they do forge social groupings and hierarchies, they differentiate between "us" and "not us" based on surface characteristics such as how another animal smells, looks, or sounds, rather than relying on abstract concepts to govern social life.

Humans, on the other hand, can make sophisticated

assumptions about the workings of the social universe, including where and how we fit into it. Our advantage is related to the fact that we possess certain mental faculties that are distinct from those of all other animals, broadly defined as consciousness. Our consciousness frees us from reliance on basic instincts and allows us to form groups on the basis of chosen preferences, values, or ideologies rather than the shared physical characteristics other primates use to determine whether another is "one of us." Our consciousness allows us to act and plan in ways that go beyond the instinctual; we may still act on instinct, but with the awareness that we are doing so. This lends us the capacity for highly advanced behavioral adaptability: in other words, the ability to modulate our behavior in order to "fit in" with everyone around us.

Consciousness then combines with language to enable cooperation, collaboration, and the transmission of sophisticated and detailed information across large groups.

Since we can never truly know how another person will behave at any moment, we have developed complex and sophisticated ways of surviving together despite having individual minds and needs. For example, the many, often conflicting, individual choices we each make when interacting in society could, in theory, cause discordant behaviors and friction. Human consciousness supplies us with shared norms and principles that inform how we must behave in order to preserve harmony in any given social interaction. In order to partake in the social flow of life, we have to learn those organizing principles and incorporate them into our everyday routines, which is the function of socialization.

In a group, mutual adherence to these organizing principles, or standards of behavior, reduces friction and provides us with a sense of togetherness. But these standards also serve another, equally important function: organizing principles allow us to process a vast number of behavioral choices at any given moment, while also ensuring a certain degree of predictability in our experiences with our fellow humans. To give a trivial example, when someone asks us for a glass of water, we can react in any one of many possible ways: we can walk away, throw the water in their face, or tell them we'd rather not. This example may seem absurd, but without clear rules about what constitutes appropriate behavior, consider the amount of information we would need to process in order to arrive at the expected result: giving the thirsty individual a glass of water.

These organizing principles can be either universal, or local.

Universal organizing principles are shared among all humans regardless of group membership or culture. We exercise restraint of impulses, we speak at a particular volume, we use recognizable facial expressions, and so forth. Those universal cues apply to everyone equally, and the assumption that everyone will abide by them provides us with a certain level of predictability even in situations that are very different from those we are accustomed to; it's how we can be relatively certain that we will not get water thrown in our face by a person who is unfamiliar to us. Social acceptance is conditioned on adherence to universal organizing rules; hence, children are expected to acquire the basics relatively quickly so as to not be shunned by their cohort.

Local organizing principles are the particular customs shared among discrete groups of people. Whether a group coheres around nationality, vocation, social class, race, religion, hobbies, politics, or any other shared identity, that group is governed by specific unwritten or even written rules. However, membership in these groups is quite fluid; the same individual often moves in and out of various circles and, in doing so, modifies their behavior according to the prevailing local principles (what a sociologist might refer to as "code switching"). When joining a new group, we need to learn these local principles quickly, even as the universal ones remain generally the same regardless of where we find ourselves.

Without organizing principles, each of us would face a deluge of choices in each and every social interaction. We would have to invest an inordinate amount of emotional energy to imagine what others think about our behavior and about us to "make sure" that we are socially okay. All our decisions and interactions would be enveloped in paralyzing doubt.

The otrovert is generally aware of universal organizing principles but often struggles to comprehend local ones, which can present challenges, the major one being that irrespective of how familiar or routine a situation is—say, walking to work in the morning, going to the neighborhood market, and even walking leisurely on the promenade or in the park—the presence of a group, even a familiar group, renders its rules unfamiliar to the otrovert. It gets even worse for otroverts when there is also a need for coordination, such as waiting in line, entering and leaving a busy department store, or weaving one's way through the crowds. I sometimes think of it like performing with a dance troupe without knowing the choreography—a situation in which one can only look anxiously at the other members and try to mimic their movements.

These organizing principles allow most people to practice "normal" behavior without apparent difficulties. But what does "normal" mean? Surprisingly, there is no consensus regarding what it takes to be considered normal, which is problematic for anyone who thinks differently. There is no clear psychiatric definition of "normal," which leaves it up to the collective to decide what and who is "abnormal."

The best definition of "normal" that I've encountered is being predictable to others. For the social contract to succeed, every member of the collective needs to meet a "threshold trust" with all the rest. And we assess trust by degrees of predictability. Predictability is generally benevolent and helpful; it is meant to ease social integration and manage the tension that can arise in a group of mingling strangers. Even though others cannot read our thoughts or foresee our intentions, we do our best to reassure them of our good intentions by behaving in a way they expect.

That is true for most interpersonal engagement in everyday life. The ability to reliably predict others' behavior enables us to go about our daily routines, over the course of which we must trust total strangers with our lives: pilots, construction engineers, physicians, drivers at a crosswalk, and so forth. Every time we consume food or drink made by another, we engage in an act of extreme trust. We unquestionably assume—with absolutely no evidence to support this assumption—that no one has poisoned it (and indeed, this trust is warranted in most instances; in its absence we would descend into paranoia).

Belonging is predicated on adhering to this sanctioned behavioral repertoire, which is why communal people are viewed as predictable and trustworthy, whereas otroverts can be met with suspicion and even fear. It makes people uncomfortable when they don't know what a non-belonger is thinking or what the non-belonger will do next (although obviously, it is not commonly possible to know what others are thinking or would do next). Those who cannot adhere to the social script decided by the majority cannot count on the trust of others.

This is the plight of otroverts: they are penalized for being unable to abandon their deepest selves for communal purposes. The power of communal suggestion requires that everyone go along with it. This means that anyone who sees reality as an individual experience may disrupt the shared perception of the rest, which is threatening to the communal order. Otroverts are made to feel weird and wrong for preferring solitude over socializing. They realize they will always be misunderstood, and even mistrusted, so they spend significant time working to create an illusion of belonging by abiding by group decorum. But following these social scripts can make routine encounters with peers maddening—and very exhausting.

These social pressures to appear "normal" and nonthreatening can combine to result in otroverts' real frustration about the need to constantly mask their real tendencies. Otroverts will do their best to follow the rules and appear predictable, but they can sustain this pretense for only so long. Because they become very good at hiding their distaste for communal events, they are often subjected to well-meaning peer pressure from those who genuinely desire their companionship or who would feel sorry for them if they "missed out" on all the fun. But other times, what might appear like the desire to spend time with them and/or spare them from FOMO is actually an unconscious attempt to validate the group. Since otroverts are nonconfrontational and conflict averse, they often cave quite easily to such peer pressure. But going against our instincts will almost always backfire. One otrovert I know told me a story of being guilted into attending her twentieth high school reunion by a friend who didn't want to go alone. She acquiesced, but about an hour into the party she had become so bored by all the small talk that she ended up leaving, slipping quietly out the back door in the hope that no one would notice. This disappearing act, she said in retrospect, "made me feel guiltier than I would have felt if I had refused to go in the first place."

This feeling of obligation is one I often encounter in my otrovert patients. One of them, J, felt highly overwhelmed. Coming from a warm, large extended family, he complained that every minute of his life was given to social obligations. Attending endless family events often left him asking himself, "What am I doing here?" On many occasions, whatever was being celebrated held little to no meaning for him. As he described one of these times, "I barely know the bridegroom; he is my second cousin on the West Coast. And yet, I had to fly to San Diego, spend the weekend in a crummy hotel, and desperately try to find something to talk about with other guests I had never met before. I hate those events."

To J, these kinds of occasions felt like entirely necessary duties (not to mention a total waste of a weekend). So together, we began to look at what turned out to be two sets of obligations: necessary ones and unnecessary ones. Necessary obligations are the things we do not want to do but have to for the sake of our careers or families, such as the less interesting or inspiring parts of a job, or attending a child's performance. Unnecessary obligations are things that we neither want nor have to do but do anyway because we feel socially pressured, such as attending multiday wedding weekends or happy hour with colleagues. When we looked deeper we found out that many of the obligations J found so draining, like that second cousin's wedding, were unnecessary. He met them begrudgingly, believing that it was his duty as a family member and that others would judge his absence harshly.

After we worked through these fears together, J realized he must choose his leisure commitments according to his own needs. It is actually that simple. Accepting invitations that we deem necessary for one reason or another is unavoidable. But there is no reason to do something solely because it is the socially dictated "thing to do." You get no accolades for attending. And the worst that can happen when you don't attend is probably some people muttering about your "asociality," but those who mutter are precisely the ones you did not want to spend time with in the first place.

Communal events were made for communal people. Many actually enjoy them, or at least find them tolerable. But this is not the case for otroverts, for whom participating in communal leisure activities—like taking an exercise class, attending a college reunion, or going on a cruise—is a kind of torture because they cannot tune out individuals in favor of the group. Events or activities that require them to follow a strict set of rules—like taking a Peloton class, joining a work task force or committee, or attending religious services—are even worse.

After years of forcing myself to attend social events, I realized that the effort invariably outweighed whatever pleasure I might have derived from the occasion. Yet, I sometimes begrudgingly go to obligations I cannot avoid, mostly regarding my children. Once, I had to attend a meet-and-greet reception with parents at my daughter's school for the start of a new year, as my wife, who normally attends such events, was abroad, and I felt I must show up for my daughter.

First, all the parents were corralled into an auditorium for a talk by the principal and the teachers. Everyone was perfectly pleasant, but I felt uncomfortable in the midst of a group that felt kinship purely because they had children at the same school in the same grade. We were organized around a superficial, and in many ways artificial, bond that made no sense to me. At the reception that followed, this shared experience made people eager to connect, which, aided by a required name tag, made me prey to unfettered small talk. It was one of those occasions when I felt I wanted to disappear—and that's what I did. I went to a faraway bathroom where I was unlikely to meet anyone and tried to calm down. Then I started feeling guilty that I was somehow damaging my daughter's success by being so childish and strange. So I returned to the party, where two or three parents standing outside the doorway beamed at me, wanting to "connect." After a few minutes, I muttered some excuses and made a beeline back to the bathroom. Now I was livid with myself. Why could I not be like all the other parents? I ran back and forth the entire evening, dodging parents, breaking away, and being drawn back. Eventually the evening ended, and I returned home exhausted and drained. Would it have been better not to have gone? Probably.

As a nonjoiner, your first duty is to yourself, and it is entirely possible to excuse yourself politely, perhaps even by telling a white lie if necessary. When J decided to follow his preferences in the way we had discussed, he immediately saw a huge improvement in his life, and no real difference for anyone else. People who liked him continued to like him and people who didn't like him continued to not like him. As for the rest, who didn't care one way or the other, well, they continued not to care. And a lot of the time, people barely even noticed. Because otroverts are so hyperaware of other individuals, we often assume that other people are the same way. But in reality, communal people are much more focused on the group than they are on the presence or absence of any individual member. In the vast majority of cases, the belief that there is some price to pay for straying from unnecessary social engagements is all in our heads.

J is far from my only patient who has tried what he did. And no one suffered any consequences other than no longer being invited to places they did not want to go in the first place—in a way the ideal outcome for otroverts. Giving ourselves permission to simply not show up is, in my experience, one of the best ways otroverts can reduce the frustration of trying to fit in, while also honoring their authentic desires and protecting their valuable time. As the English philosopher and politician John Stuart Mill once wrote, "The danger which threatens human nature is not the excess, but the deficiency, of personal impulses and preferences."

PART III

THE VIRTUES OF BEING AN OTROVERT

10

Emotional Self-Sufficiency

I t is an inescapable fact that all humans are born, live, and die alone. Surrounding ourselves with others makes it possible to deny that fact. Group membership allows communal people to convince themselves that theirs is a shared fate, whereas being alone can remind them of their true, solitary destiny, which, for most, is an uncomfortable and even intolerable reality to accept. The otrovert, on the other hand, does not feel part of a shared fate. Because being alone is intrinsic to their lifelong experience, otroverts feel comfortable in their solitude.

However, in a group, the otrovert cannot help but feel very lonely. Most of the discomfort originates from trying to fit in and play a role that is expected of them, a performance otroverts find exhausting. When togetherness is reassuring and pleasant, sacrificing energy for it makes sense. For otroverts, that energy is twice wasted: one, the group's presence does not bring a sense of reassurance, and two, it is not pleasant. Once otroverts understand and embrace their need for solitude, however, they are able to tune out the expectations of the group and instead tune in to themselves.

Members of a collective must be mindful of the other members' approval or disapproval of them, and people almost universally prefer to be liked rather than disliked. This may result from the push toward communality in early life, when we learn to associate the approving smiles of our caregivers with food, safety, and all else that a helpless infant needs to survive. Even at this early age, we discover that we will be rewarded with affection and approval for relinquishing the instinctive self-centered attitude we are born with and doing what is expected of us.

In adulthood, the desire to blend in and be accepted by the rest, the need for recognition from our peers, and the constant "negotiation of needs" required to win the affection of other group members entail a deeper level of sacrifice that most are unaware of: the progressive loss of emotional self-reliance.

The otrovert, untethered from the collective, can distinguish between the gravitational pull of the group and their inner, personal center of gravity. They are not afraid to think the "wrong" thoughts or experience the "wrong" feelings, as they do not measure what is right or wrong against any communal yardstick. Because they don't require group validation, they are inherently self-sufficient: they rarely experience self-recrimination or self-loathing, and they never shame or guilt others.

TRUSTING ONE'S INSTINCTS

As life unfolds, otroverts learn to trust themselves in personal decisions. They know themselves and what they need to make their
life as pleasant and productive as possible. They see themselves for
who they are and know what they can and cannot do well. When,
for example, they do a great job on a work presentation, they know
it. They don't ruminate about how they did or wait for someone to
tell them they did a great job and then wonder whether the person
meant it. This self-awareness and self-reliance helps them be deci-
sive, willful, and confident in choosing directions in life.

As a novelist, Franz Kafka created an unforgettable portrayal
of how the otrovert mindset manifests in the larger world.[1] In
books like The Trial, The Metamorphosis, The Castle, and others, he presented worlds in which belonging was considered the
instinctive, "natural" way to be, written from the often bewildered
perspective of people who are persecuted for their inability to fit in.

But Kafka could also be much gentler in shining a light on
the vast limitations of the belonger's mindset. For instance, in his
short story "Josephine the Singer, or the Mouse Folk," he describes
the workings of the hive mind with sublime, wry humor, through
the story of a mouse society struggling to decipher the talents of a
mouse named Josephine, a famous singer. But despite her celebrity,
it turns out that Josephine does not actually have any particular

---

1 Franz Kafka, "Josephine the Singer, or the Mouse Folk," A Hunger Artist (Berlin:
Verlag die Schmiede, 1924).

musical talent. Like all the other mice, she is merely whistling with no distinction. She is considered to be a sublime singer only because the society has decided to adore her; the belief that she is special and unique results from the surrender of individual perception to the collective adulation.

Kafka presents this submission to the group's dictum as the logical consequence of the "terribly bleak and difficult" life the mice live, one that affords no interest in or time for sublime pastimes like art and music. Alone, a mouse has no reprieve from its troubles, but sitting together, listening to Josephine's performance, the mice can forget their individual misery and experience a shared pleasure. "Being carried along day and night upon the shoulders of the community," Kafka writes, is an attractive proposition for people who are conditioned to fear being alone.

For communal people, succumbing to collective wishes is easy, and resisting peer pressure is very hard. Otroverts are the exact opposite, as evidenced by an otrovert patient of mine when she got embroiled in a painful custody battle with her abusive husband, who was refusing to pay child support. Even when things got ugly, she continued to fight, goaded on by her lawyers and by all her friends and family members, who constantly praised her for standing her ground since she was very clearly in the right. At long last, they reminded her, she had the opportunity to make him pay for all the years of abuse, adding that this war of attrition against him was essential to "teach him a lesson." Her mother kept telling her, "What doesn't kill you will make you stronger," but she told me, "I don't feel I am getting stronger. It feels the other way around—in a way it is killing me."

I gave her the advice I give to my otrovert patients in similar situations: Just walk away. No money or revenge is worth your peace of mind. On the otrovert's list of priorities, peace of mind ranks high. They are unable to accommodate toxic behavior and have a deep aversion to conflict and confrontation. Rather than surrender, most otroverts simply refuse to engage in a fight to begin with. Being noncompetitive makes losing or winning inconsequential.

My patient felt a tremendous sense of relief and decided to follow my advice, which was consistent with her own feelings about the court case. Predictably, her family and friends were upset with her decision and the lawyers thought she was making a grave mistake, but she followed her heart and refused to abide by their advice. She came away feeling strong for sticking by her convictions and prioritizing her own sanity rather than weak for giving in to her ex.

THE NEED FOR SOLITUDE

In his diaries, Kafka wrote, "Being alone has a power over me that never fails. My interior dissolves (for the time being, only superficially) and is ready to release what lies deeper. When I am willfully alone, a slight ordering of my interior begins to take place, and I need nothing more."

I cannot think of a better description of the relief and satisfaction an otrovert experiences when retreating into their true self.

Even when communal people are alone, they are not completely disconnected from the group; they are apart from them while continuing to be influenced by them. When an otrovert is alone, they are absolutely alone. They do not compare their thoughts with anyone else's, wonder whether their behaviors are socially accepted, or think about what other people might be doing at that moment and why they weren't included. This freedom from external influences gives them the mental space to formulate original and imaginative ideas.

As we have seen, being an otrovert in a world that rewards joiners is not without its difficulties. The good news is that these challenges are far outweighed by the strengths that otroverts possess. While Kafka produced some of his most creative work "in solitude"—where he was able to tap into "this tremendous world I have inside of me"—he also understood that dwelling in his inner world need not result in alienation and estrangement; that one's inner world could be recognized and embraced as a guide to designing the full, happy, and productive life that most otroverts achieve.

This emotional self-reliance is among the great gifts of non-belonging, but there are many others as well.

11

Empathy and Connection

Otroverts are not misanthropes. In fact, people are fascinating to otroverts, and even if they cannot feel an affinity for or sense of belonging within the group as a unit, they are still able to bond one-on-one with each individual within it (as we have seen, this is one way in which otroverts differ from introverts, loners, and those with autism). D. H. Lawrence described this otrovert tendency this way: "Perhaps only people who are capable of real togetherness have that look of being alone in the universe. The others have a certain stickiness; they stick to the mass."

When it comes to friendship, otroverts prefer quality over quantity. Though they cannot fathom how a group thinks collectively, have trouble fitting into the social ecosystems of their workplaces and communities, and don't understand the pleasure taken in shared activities or the bonhomie that communal people find so comforting, a very good friend or two, and perhaps a long-term partner, satisfy the otrovert's need for connection and company.

While many communal people are fair-weather friends—there for the good times but likely to disappear when you really need them—an otrovert is always available to their friends when they are needed, without expectation of reciprocity. Because the otrovert is incapable of the social jockeying and mind games that so many communal people learn to employ, no one ever has to doubt their motives; when they are kind and generous, it is because they find helping others rewarding.

MEANINGFUL COMMUNICATION

Because otroverts are both curious and friendly, they can strike up deep conversations with people during relatively brief encounters; in fact, this is the only way they know how to communicate. They cannot bear small talk, which the anthropologist Bronislaw Malinowski, who was the first to research the social function of small talk, described as "purposeless expressions of preference or aversions, accounts of irrelevant happenings, [and] comments on what is perfectly obvious."

Most people are made very uncomfortable by silence, especially in the company of people they don't know, and so many fill the void with chitchat that is meant to establish only superficial connection and provides no common ground for meaningful communication. Otroverts, on the other hand, plunge right ahead with the "genuine stuff," as L, an otrovert friend of mine, describes it. In casual encounters with strangers, L is very friendly and warm. Often, the other person will feel a connection to him that goes beyond what would be expected from casual small talk, and may even try to continue the connection by suggesting they meet again. When L politely declines, and they realize that the warm friendliness was not a prelude to friendship—the otrovert's threshold for whom they consider a friend is quite high—but simply a pleasant conversation in its own right, some are baffled as to how they misread the signs. Others get upset and recoil at what they consider an affront or even a betrayal.

L's preferred conversational partners are those who respond to his attempts to dispatch with small talk in kind and join his immediate dive into deeper topics. But to the otrovert, even deep conversation does not have to be a prelude to a deep relationship. It can be enjoyed for what it is: a genuine exchange of opinions and points of view.

Communal people have been conditioned to believe that small talk is a prerequisite for a polite social encounter; it is only otroverts who understand that it is possible to be friendly without engaging in superficial exchanges. A colleague of mine recalls how it took her mother, a first-generation immigrant and otrovert, upwards of a decade living in America to get used to the absurd (in her view) exchange of pleasantries when interacting with store clerks and other strangers. "Why is she asking me how I'm doing today? She doesn't even know me," she would grumble about the friendly cashier at the grocery store the moment she was out of earshot.

Beyond small talk, the otrovert finds absurdity in any social ritual to which the group has arbitrarily assigned a sense of shared importance (generally speaking, Albert Camus's notion of life itself as absurd is very compatible with otrovert perception). For example, settings in which people tend to take on an air of artificial seriousness or self-importance—like the opera or an avant-garde art show—are cringeworthy to the otrovert. They cannot partake in rituals or ceremonies where there is a silent agreement among group members that this is a solemn moment and everyone is expected to play their role. That these rituals are important simply because the group has deemed them so does not compute for the otrovert.

There is a nice story in Judaism about a village fool who is so overwhelmed by the services on Yom Kippur that he puts two fingers in his mouth and whistles loudly just as the rabbi is about to blow the shofar. The congregation is horrified and starts scolding the embarrassed man. But the rabbi says, "No, let him be. He whistled because that is how he can express his religious fervor. In fact, by his earnest act, he has opened the gate to heaven, so we do not need to blow the shofar this year." The otrovert understands that rituals have no inherent meaning beyond that with which we collectively imbue them, and that by assuming that there is a particular "right" way to act out that meaning, we sometimes diminish it. Otroverts are very close to their beliefs and feelings but prefer to express them on their own time and in their own way.

HUMOR AND CHARISMA

To manage their intolerance for what they consider "unimportant seriousness," the otrovert will often become silly and jocular. In some cases, this can derail serious conversations or be seen as a sign of disrespect for solemn moments; in others, it can provide a fresh breath of levity and catharsis exactly when it is needed most. Being a perpetual observer rather than a true participant lends the otrovert a particularly strong radar for spotting the absurd in everyday life, which can be great fodder for humor.

Though otroverts can be as entertaining as stand-up comics, focusing on the absurdity in the mundane and getting big laughs from people who will nonetheless continue to behave the same as always, they never "punch down." They might poke fun at established norms or power structures but prefer self-deprecating humor and ridiculing themselves to make a point. This is how they deploy humor with both empathy and charm.

12

Confidence and Contentment

Otroverts don't need permission, approval, validation, or adulation in the way that communal people do. Needing to convince no one of the "correctness" of their decisions or actions saves them from many unnecessary conversations and distractions.

Because they are not governed by the persistent need to be liked, they are able to set clear boundaries to protect their mental energy and time. They are the ultimate decision-makers of what is frivolous and what is productive—and they make time for both.

Status is always something measured relative to other people within a social grouping, and because otroverts are not tethered to such a group, they never look to others to measure the value of their choices, lifestyle, or possessions. This also means they live without FOMO (recall the story from chapter 1 of my patient's son, whose mother was unduly worried about his missing out on social experiences). Because their decisions are their own, unswayed by outside influences, otroverts are quite content with their choices. They can like and be comfortable with who they are without the need for external validation.

This disinterest in winning the adulation of the collective is exemplified in the casual way Kafka treated his literary vocation. It is telling that one of the greatest literary giants in human history spent so little time trying to publish or call attention to his writings, and even went so far as to ask in his will that his work be destroyed after his death. When his friend and executor, Max Brod, went against his wishes, he did a great service to humanity but a disservice to Kafka, who did not write for the purpose of recognition; he wrote simply because he wanted to.

Due to their lack of FOMO and their disinterest in markers of status, otroverts generally don't feel envious of others' financial successes, couldn't care less about keeping up with the Joneses, and do not usually covet what they do not have. They view earning money as a source of safety—a means to make life easier rather than a goal—so they often have quite different financial and vocational priorities from those of the group. They tend to be unhappy and unsuccessful if they try to work solely for the purpose of earning money, though those who can choose a career curated to their talent and motivation are often financially successful and fulfilled by their work. They are unlikely to compromise their lifestyle to get something they don't feel they need.

This doesn't mean otroverts are necessarily ascetic or frugal. While being clear on what they do and don't need leads to a narrow, carefully chosen set of material possessions, many otro-verts love luxury—particularly the ability to distance themselves from the multitudes that it offers. For example, one otrovert I know lives a modest lifestyle but will always splurge on first-class plane tickets; she is willing to pay an exorbitant premium not for legroom or the three-course meal but for a modicum of additional privacy and distance from fellow passengers.

THE ULTIMATE AUTHORITY ON THEIR OWN LIFE

Otroverts don't like taking advice from anyone short of profession-als who know things the otrovert does not. However, otroverts do not accept advice on something they already have all the neces-sary information about: themselves.

Often, the goal of belonging is at odds with the goal of engag-ing with the world in ways that support rather than diminish who we are. Being part of a communal group with its awesome gravity can lead to self-effacement, or at least to confusion between one's true desires and what the group wants. To be in charge of your life and relationships, you must have a strong private self that takes the needs of the group into account but does not succumb to the communal echo chamber. Most people are excited to discover this self and learn how to balance what they want and need with the pleasures and support they find in shared concerns, passions, and occupations. For others, it has been so long since they considered their individual needs that they've forgotten how to differentiate their true wants and wishes from the implicit requirements for membership and acceptance within a collective. In our pluralist society, belonging requires continually making adjustments to bring our choices more in line with our desires.

When the boundary between the individual and the group dissipates, the ability to distinguish between what you want and what the group wants goes with it. Such was the case for my patient S when she joined a retirement community, partially on my advice. Recently widowed, with both of her children living three thousand miles away with their families, she decided to relocate. She welcomed the idea of community living—she had always been outgoing and friendly and was not worried about fitting in or finding friends. She chose an elegant gated community where she would have a house of her own, large enough for her children and grandchildren to visit. Personally, I would have made a very different choice, but her "what can go wrong?" attitude convinced me she had made the right decision.

Then, about three months after she had relocated, she called me in tears, saying, "I cannot stand being here." Because seniors are so prone to becoming isolated, her new community put great stock in togetherness. The days were filled with group activities: meals, book clubs, yoga classes, and many other social opportunities. The problem was that the pressure to participate in these activities was suffocating; everyone in the community put pressure on everyone else to join, to make sure that no one ever stayed home alone. In addition, because she was a widow, the neighbors assumed she wanted to meet men and were constantly introducing her to widowers. "It's a living hell for me," was how she described it, "and the worst part is that my reluctance to attend any activity is viewed as a sign that I'm withdrawing, which makes them double their efforts to 'assimilate' me." She was well aware that all these people were kind and had only good intentions, but she realized they valued togetherness in a way she did not. She regretted trading the ability to be alone in the big city for this mandatory togetherness. Fortunately, her apartment had just gone on the market, and she was able to pull it back, giving her time to rethink her decision to relocate. One thing was certain, though: she should not go back to the gated community, surrounded by people so used to being together that they had lost the ability to distinguish the individual from the collective.

Communal people derive enough joy from being together that it compensates for the loss of their personal agency. But this is not the case for otroverts like S, for whom that line between the self and others was never blurred.

Because otroverts take sole ownership of their responsibilities and decisions, they're always working to minimize negative consequences and bad memories, leading to rational decisions that make sense for them. For example, I like to take walks on narrow country roads, but I am always very careful to make sure drivers can see me clearly; I can never understand those who simply assume that drivers surely see them. The reluctance to trust strangers with my life or well-being makes me risk averse but also provides inner calm.

Being the ultimate authority in their own lives, otroverts do not rely on the kind of reality check the hive employs to inform their perspectives or preferences. What seems obvious to the rest may not seem obvious to otroverts, and vice versa. Unfazed by social trends, otroverts usually develop their own style of living and stay faithful to it. They remain unmoved by consumerist pressures, advertising, and starred reviews or other common ranking and rating methods that shape collective preferences, and are unlikely to fall for scams or fad treatments—even when recommended by a credentialed doctor—that make no sense to them.

Because they decide on their own what makes sense rather than relying on group opinion, all information must pass the sensical/nonsensical filter in their mind. Invariably, this mechanism becomes dominant in their everyday encounters. Though they need more time than the average person to digest information, this process frees them to form opinions on what they *want* to understand, rather than passively absorb the majority's take on current events, culture, and everything else.

Most people spend too much time worrying about how they come across to their coworkers and supervisors, their friends and neighbors, sometimes even their own family members. Even more of their precious mental energy is then expended wondering what is the appropriate thing to do, the appropriate thing to say, and whom to speak with according to local decorum. But the otrovert wastes little time or energy thinking about such social conventions. As John Lennon famously said, "Life is what happens to you while you're busy making other plans." Otroverts are not busy making other plans or wondering about others' plans. They live very powerfully in the here and now.

Accustomed to being masters of their own time, otroverts can be quite impatient in situations they can't control. They can't stand having to endure certain inconveniences other people grudgingly accept as part of life—particularly those that result from hive mind behavior, such as a traffic jam formed because all the other drivers on the road were rubbernecking at a fender bender; waiting in an interminable line at the DMV behind people who showed up without the proper documentation; or missing a flight because of passengers' unruly behavior at the security gate. I personally can never understand people who voluntarily choose to stand in line for anything. For communal people, a long line—be it for concert tickets, a table at a popular restaurant, or the grand opening of a new art exhibit—signals something that must be worth waiting for. To otroverts like me, it feels like a complete waste of time.

As an immigrant father who had lived my entire life without ever holding a baseball in my hands, I felt the need when my son was younger to do something that I thought was a rite of passage for American kids: take him to Disneyland. We bought VIP tickets to try to avoid having to wait in the notoriously long lines but then felt too guilty to use them once we saw all the eager children who would be forced to wait even longer to go on the ride. After thirty minutes, my then four-year-old said, "Daddy, if we leave now we can still say we went to Disneyland." Elated, I completely agreed, and we walked out with a sense of accomplishment.

13

Thinking Outside the Hive

In the early 1990s, I had the opportunity to run a schizophrenia unit at Mount Sinai Hospital in Manhattan that was affiliated with a long-term psychiatric state hospital. There were many patients there termed "treatment nonresponders," who ended up staying locked in this hospital for the rest of their lives after failing to respond to treatment. I had a great deal of sympathy for their plight and would go to the hospital once a week to find patients interested in reevaluating their treatment. Most of them were hopeless and had given up on the prospect of doing better. Many were besieged by hallucinations and delusions, which meant they were too sick to give informed consent. The prevailing opinion was that these patients didn't respond to treatment because something about their constitution was different, so we looked for structural brain differences, metabolic issues, and other conditions that could alter the effects of medications. In the vast majority of cases, we came up empty-handed.

Based on my experience with those patients, I began to be burdened by a growing concern that my colleagues and I were trapped in a cognitive distortion. Perhaps these 20 percent of psychiatric patients were nonresponsive not because something in *them* was wrong but because the *treatment* was wrong. In other words, perhaps they had different conditions than the ones they were being treated for. In psychiatry, individual variables are often overlooked once a diagnosis has been assigned. Patients are swiftly admitted into a group of similarly diagnosed patients, who are eventually divided into two groups: those who "respond" and those who do not "respond" to a certain medication regimen.

Intellectually, I understood why things were done this way. Clinical studies demand a large number of participants, and grouping people according to the symptoms they have in common is much more efficient than looking for the ways in which their symptoms are different. Yet, in my mind's eye, no matter how large a clinical trial, I still see a group of individuals. It was clear that I could not run a study of treatment nonresponders by examining how each individual differed from every other individual in the test group. But I couldn't help but share my idea with anyone who cared to listen—my students, my colleagues, and even my patients' family members. It was evident to me that the lack of a response to medication that works for similarly diagnosed patients meant that there was a mismatch between medication and diagnosis, yet the "normal" way of dealing with those patients who remained symptomatic was to make them wait for "new and improved" versions of the medication they were not responding to.

This completely flawed logic meant that thousands of patients languished in locked facilities for years, and more often than not, if some new drug did come along, they were passed over for it, as the institutions where they lived were more interested in keeping the patients calm (often with a large dose of tranquilizers) than they were in actually treating them. Once a nonresponder was committed to a long-term-care institution, they would have little to no chance for an active, ongoing review of their condition; no efforts would be made to further investigate why the "right" medications were eliciting the wrong responses (in this case, no response at all) or to revisit their diagnosis periodically with new perspectives born of advances in psychiatry and medicine during the decades they had spent locked up in a hospital. Reevaluating each of the nonresponding patients' conditions seemed like an insurmountable task. Having no support from the institutions, I moved on to other projects, though I couldn't stop thinking and talking about my idea to study nonresponders to anyone willing to listen.

Two years later, I was walking in Midtown Manhattan when I bumped into a friend who was the director of that same psychiatric state hospital that I had visited weekly. A hospital administrator with no medical background, she had then already been deeply dedicated to the patients under her charge. She and I used to take coffee breaks with some of her staff, and I would tell them about my idea of giving nonresponding patients a second chance. When

I ran into her two years later, she was on her way to lunch and suggested I join her. There, she told me she had recently been promoted to associate commissioner in the Office of Mental Health, the New York State agency overseeing all the mental health activities around the state. I told her I was very happy for her promotion, and I was; it is wonderful when such talented and dedicated people are recognized. Then she asked me, "What's going on with your second-chance program?"

I told her about the obstacles—academic, financial, administrative, and more—I had encountered in trying to find a place to test my hypothesis. She said, "I think I have a way. But it would require a great sacrifice on your part." She then went on to explain that her state agency was looking for a young and passionate medical director for operations and asked if I would agree to meet the state commissioner and consider the position. I knew that she shared my propensity to "think outside the box," and the thought of working together suddenly revived the second-chance idea as a real possibility.

The next week, I met with the commissioner of mental health. He was a lovely, highly intelligent, and gentle person, and I liked him from the first moment. He was not a physician but a seasoned social worker who had risen from the trenches and was very familiar with the system. I gave an impromptu presentation of my rationale and strategy for the second-chance program, and he said, "I like your way of thinking. We need you in Albany." I was still hesitant, as the idea of commuting two and a half hours to Albany was daunting. "I hope you will accept the position," he said, adding jokingly, "You may not have a second chance to carry out the program." He was right. This was a unique, unsolicited, one-time opportunity. This fortunate coincidence, in the chance meeting with my friend on the street, would never repeat itself. I had to do it. I accepted under the condition that I would not relocate to Albany but stay with my family in Manhattan, commuting weekly instead. I never regretted it.

The transition was smooth, but the job was enormous in scope, and I barely lifted my head to breathe for a year. The difficulties and obstacles were many and various, including regulatory, financial, strategic, and staffing problems. Then there was the background drumbeat of naysayers among psychiatrists who were trapped in the aforementioned groupthink. My proposal to revisit each patient's diagnosis and symptoms for different treatment strategies rather than looking for version 2.0 of the same treatments seemed antagonistic to the prevailing ethos. Which was, in a sense, exactly the point.

The first patient arrived at the academic psychiatric hospital twenty-two years ago, and the Second Chance Program has been in existence ever since. At the outset, we worked with those who had been hospitalized for a median time of twenty years. Many of those people had lost any ability to function on their own—a direct result of many years spent locked in a psychiatric unit with other severely ill patients and no responsibilities, agency, or path toward a better life. Some patients, we soon discovered, were not mentally ill at all, but had been admitted at a time when knowledge about various other conditions, such as Tourette's syndrome, was limited. Most patients had never used any electronic devices, did not know how to shop, how to make food, how to do their laundry, or how to perform the myriad other activities of daily living that most people consider routine and trivial. Now they had to learn or relearn those skills, along with how to use public transportation, pay bills, show up for appointments, and interact with strangers in a way they hadn't done since they were admitted. Each patient who recovered symptomatically but was too broken to master the skills needed to live independently got a place in a program that offered protective living as well as a full range of social and medical services. Since then, hundreds of patients have been transitioned back into the community.

Though it has been many years since I left that government position, to this day few moments bring me more joy than when I sit with my young residents and they say, "This patient seems like a good candidate for the Second Chance Program. Are you familiar with that?" At which point I smile under my mustache and answer, "Yes, to a certain extent," and let them tell me about it.

Starting this program is perhaps my most enduring legacy, and my proudest example of what can be achieved by working around the status quo. I will admit that for many years before actually launching the program, I succumbed to everyone telling me my idea was both impossible and futile. This would be the last time I would allow a figure of authority—or anyone—to make me believe that I was wrong just because no one else thought I was right. It showed me definitively that we (unfortunately) live in a culture that puts sticking with the consensus opinion above all else, even when that means depriving victims of a broken system of a second chance to participate in life. And it solidified my conviction that our society desperately needs more perspectives and ideas that do not conform to the conventional wisdom dictated by the hive mind.

THE ABSTRACTIONS OF THE COLLECTIVE MIND

Emily Dickinson once wrote, "The soul selects her own society." Yet for many souls, one's position in society is not so much a choice as it is a function of where we live, what family, religion, or social class we were born into, and what ethnicity and/or race we are. Most people embrace—or at least accept—the social groups to which they have been assigned. Otroverts do not. They place no trust in any group formed around an abstract idea or circumstance of birth, such as ideology, politics, race, economy, religion, and nationality, which exist only in the collective mind. For them, the idea of unquestionable devotion to a group of people linked by a set of tacit criteria agreed upon by the group's members makes little sense, no matter how venerable that group is in the eyes of the majority.

Most humans adhere to these binding abstractions for various reasons—many of them completely valid. Membership in a group of people who share our ideology, background, or aspects of our experience creates a path for connection, which is especially appealing when other obvious routes, such as family or work, aren't available. Such groups also provide a set of unwritten instructions about how to behave, which helps to ward off ambiguity and uncertainty, while also keeping everyone in line. When things are good, these affiliations provide a sense of shared identity, and with it a crude way of determining who is a friend to be trusted and who is a foe to be feared. And when things are bad, as mentioned earlier, the group ethos becomes hugely important in deciding how best to navigate the crisis and what might need to be sacrificed in its name. Though we no longer need to be part of a tribe to survive predators or the threats of the natural world, most people do still need it to survive the very experience of being human. Unlike most herd animals, which cooperate passively, humans can cooperate actively by creating a notional entity based on many people agreeing to share the same opinions and beliefs. A hive mind creates "collective intelligence" or "communal wisdom" by pooling experiential resources. Most of us learn to conform because belonging to or participating in the hive mind provides illusory protection: the belief in strength in numbers. And as the group's size increases, the demands for conformity intensify, as it cements the unity necessary for the group's rule. This urge to belong subsumes all that is distinctive about a person once they become a member of the hive.

For most people, this sacrifice is made easily and instinctively. Not so for otroverts, who are neither willing nor able to passively adopt the social scripts that others do. To the otrovert, who is constantly engaged with the choices and consequences of their individual life, social norms follow a circular logic: the reason people follow them is because they have been widely accepted, and the reason they have been widely accepted is because many people follow them. To highlight the arbitrary nature of such rules, an otrovert might put it this way: If you were stranded alone on a desert island, would you still value everything that you value or were taught to value? Or would you realize that most of these judgments are useful and relevant only in the context of other humans?

Non-belonging is kind of like living life on an island, while belongers are on the mainland. When otroverts visit the mainland, they pay attention to the prevailing rules and try their best to abide by them, but they are always accidental tourists there. The rules are of no use to them elsewhere.

Otroverts cannot be convinced of the validity of an idea sheerly through the number of people who hold it. It is the idea itself that matters. The tools of the hive mind—consensus, majority, communal wisdom, and experience that come down through the generations—are useless to the otrovert if the concept behind the idea seems wrong to them. On the other hand, a wise observation or statement made by someone, irrespective of position or authority, can be profoundly appreciated by an otrovert if it strikes them as true.

As a very young man, I had my heart broken. Nothing anyone said—none of the usual platitudes—provided any source of comfort. Then a Bedouin waiter in a tea shop I frequented said to me, "A broken heart is like a burn. At first, it hurts all the time, then only when you touch it, and eventually, it does not hurt at all. There might be only a faded scar to remind you." This was forty-five years ago. He was very right, and I still impart Wadid's wisdom to others.

FREETHINKING AND ORIGINALITY

Belongingness and consensus do not lend themselves to originality. Unencumbered by the hive mind, otroverts are original thinkers. They see what everyone else sees, but because they are not subordinate to the gravitational pull of groupthink, they allow themselves to ponder alternative interpretations. And due in part to their disinterest in popular culture and other mass entertainment, they have the mental space to embark regularly on intellectual adventures fueled by introspection and creativity. This opens the possibility of stumbling on serendipitous observations that elude the collective. Because they stray from the prevailing thinking, their ideas often seem radical or even threatening. This is true of virtually all truly original thinkers throughout human history, both the famous ones we have all heard of and the ones lost to the annals of the past.

Dr. Ignaz Semmelweis, a Hungarian physician, falls in the second category. In 1861, he published a book called *The Etiology, Concept, and Prophylaxis of Childbed Fever,* which described his research on maternal death during childbirth from what we now call puerperal fever. His conclusion, revolutionary for those times, was that these deaths could be prevented merely by doctors washing their hands before assisting in delivery. Nowadays, it is obvious that medical procedures should be performed under sterile and clean conditions to prevent contamination, but germs and their putative role in infection were unknown in his day. Dr. Semmelweis deduced the connection in what was then an unconventional way: by visiting a delivery clinic where the women who gave birth were contracting childbed fever in significantly lower numbers.

Upon observing the midwives who ran this clinic, he found only one difference in their methods: many of the doctors at the hospital assisted with labor immediately after performing autopsies, while the midwives didn't. He concluded that the physicians might be transferring what he called "organic material" (i.e., germs and bacteria) from the autopsy to the delivery via their hands and suggested that they wash carefully before delivering a baby. Though deeply skeptical that something so trivial as handwashing could make a measurable difference, the doctors took his suggestion. When they did, the maternal death rate at the hospital immediately dropped from 18 percent to 2 percent.

Dr. Semmelweis knew nothing about bacteria and their role in infection; he simply saw something that no one else in the clinics was able to see, and this single insight was enough to profoundly alter the horrible reality of the many women dying from infection. Like most innovations, though, Semmelweis's discovery was received very poorly by his colleagues. Even after the success of his intervention had been clearly demonstrated, they demanded a theoretical explanation as to why handwashing reduced mortality, something that Semmelweis could not provide. He was shunned by the medical society, was fired from his clinical and academic positions, and suffered an emotional breakdown. His colleagues then committed him to an asylum, where he was beaten by the orderlies. He died ten days later from sepsis caused by his dirty wounds (the irony is very poignant), at the age of forty-seven.[2]

The ideas that emerge from the otrovert mind carry the risk of being viewed as subversive, heretic, or even insane, even when the evidence clearly suggests otherwise.

In a society governed by the communal order, the otrovert's way of thinking is threatening. But at a time when the challenges we face as a society require us to question conventional assumptions, contemplate problems from new perspectives, and open our minds to unorthodox solutions, the otrovert's way of thinking also has the power to change the world.

MEMORY AND TIME

The hive mind exists primarily in the present, fueled by an incessant interest in the zeitgeist: news, politics, popular culture, and gossip are the building blocks for shared experience. Along with this comes relative disinterest in yesterday's news; to stay mentally synchronized as a single group, everyone within that group has to

---

2   Howard Markel, "In 1850, Ignaz Semmelweis Saved Lives with Three Words: Wash Your Hands," PBS.org, May 15, 2015.

keep shifting their attention to the next thing, which is why the hive mind has a perpetual shared interest in the now.

It is worth adding that focusing on the *shared* now should not be confused with mindfulness, as mindfulness is exercised individually. Whereas the hive mind considers the present through the lens of shared experience, it considers the past through shared memories, myths, fables, and traditions, each one a thread in the collective historical context that often dwarfs any individual's personal past. Similarly, plans for the future are largely dictated by the collective doctrine of what is wrong, right, appropriate, or worthy. The same occurs when it comes to collective deliberations regarding the consequences of current actions. If this were not the case, it would be impossible to understand how each generation can repeat anew the grave mistakes of the past and be surprised by the "unintended" consequences.

Untethered from the hive mind, otroverts perceive their place in history and time differently. Their personal experience of the present moment is not linked to that of all the other people who are also experiencing it, and their memories of the past are not clouded by the collective narrative. Because of their minimal connection to contemporary culture, mores, trends, and so on, their memories are more personal and rarely contemporaneous with those of any other human. If you asked a group of people to recount their memories of a particular moment in time, many of them would likely cite the song that was always playing on the radio or the style of clothing that was in vogue, whereas otroverts would recount a specific experience they had had.

Otroverts, in other words, focus not on collective memory but on the self and their personal voyage through time. As a result, the otrovert's sense of time is longitudinal: today is an outcome of yesterday, and tomorrow is a consequence of today. Every moment, and every memory, is as precious as the last.

14

The Richness of Inner Life

When I work with patients, I see my role as that of a sherpa who can guide them in navigating terrifying terrain they wouldn't dare to explore alone. I am referring here to their inner lives.

This confrontation with the self is frightening and overwhelming for most people. Because no one has access to our inner thoughts, our inner world is the one place where we are truly, unavoidably alone. And so, because as social animals we tend to feel discomfort with aloneness, most humans deal with their inner world by paying little attention to it. But as with most relationships in life, neglecting our relationship with our inner world brings malfunction, as insights that could have better connected our experience with our deeper knowledge of ourselves are lost.

As a result, we base many decisions (consciously or not) on a faulty, incomplete set of data. We expect to be able to rely on our instincts—or what we call "a gut feeling"—for the most important, intimate decisions, but because we don't pay attention to our instincts most of the time, calling on them in urgent moments can steer us wrong. In the absence of a strong internal compass, we confuse the "communal wisdom" for our own personally informed common sense. And when our inner convictions, values, and preferences come into conflict with those of the collective, we learn to abandon or suppress them to align with the hive and win social acceptance.

Eventually the inner world is so inaccessible and incomprehensible that it becomes a burden. We might call this burnout, midlife crisis, or depression. But in truth it's the result of closing ourselves off to our most private thoughts and dreams and desires, which we are conditioned to believe can be wrong or inappropriate or selfish, even if we never act upon them. The sense of awe that came naturally to us as children gets squeezed out of us, leaving us no choice but to conjure or feign enthusiasm for what the group considers awesome. It's no wonder people look for psychedelics to probe the depths of their inner experience; they're bored with the ersatz imagination the group feeds them.

For most people, the commingling of the physical world, the communal world, and their inner world creates fluid boundaries between the self and others. Otroverts, on the other hand, have a strong demarcation between the two. They know it's possible to exist in both their inner and outer worlds—but they are hyperaware of the boundary between them. They cannot access the autopilot mode that allows communal people to drift between these two worlds and flow in oblivious harmony with the rest.

This disconnect between the self and the other comes with real benefits. It is why otroverts are able to tune out many of the concerns that occupy communal people, like envy and shame, and instead tune in to themselves. Tuned in to their rich, multilayered inner worlds, they gain access to a fantastically complex universe of thought, memory, and imagination that the communal person cannot access.

To my patients who extol the virtue of psychedelic trips I say, I can reach the same experiences without drugs, as I never lost access to the psychedelic aspect of my imagination. Unlike those who have abandoned their inner world to dwell permanently in the communal realm, otroverts prefer the complexity of their inner worlds to the shallow interactions and pedestrian concerns that preoccupy the collective.

Many communal people are so fearful of exposing their deepest dreams and desires, they will attempt to take the rules of the social world we live in and apply them to their inner lives as well. For example, let's say I envy someone for his sports car. As an otrovert, chances are that I won't even express those feelings aloud, much less act on them. Otroverts understand that their inner mind is private, and they protect this privacy by ensuring that their deepest feelings are made public only to the extent they decide to share them. But I also won't deny these feelings to myself, nor will I feel bad about having them. I feel perfectly free to indulge all my most covetous and (some would say) unattractive instincts in my own mind. As a result, I am not tortured by them.

But a communal person, whose boundary between their inner and outer worlds is much more porous, does not want their less attractive instincts—like petty envy or jealousy—laid bare to the world and often feels guilty, embarrassed, or ashamed for things they cannot control in their inner dialogue. To be free of this impulse means abandoning the idea of trying to police their innermost emotions or urges. Simply knowing that one's inner world is not subject to the rules of societal decorum is immensely liberating, as is the idea that thoughts and feelings cannot be wrong or right, if only because we cannot control them.

Most universal rules of **interpersonal** behavior are handed down and maintained by society at large, requiring no input from you. Our inner, **intrapersonal** governing principles are another matter. Your inner world is a place where you can think whatever you want, so long as you don't act it out and don't try to convince others of it. You're not beholden to any social mores, because they are designed to govern your interactions with others. You are, in the most profound sense, free.

LANGUAGE AND THE PSYCHE

When interacting with the social world, we all use words that condense the richness of our emotional experience to sound bites. Communal people are typically content to live in a world where every thought and sentiment has been reduced and simplified for ease of consumption and efficiency of communication. This is a world where a feeling like love is turned into a universal term that is just as likely to be used to describe how we feel about a car, an old pair of shoes, or our job as it is to describe our feelings about our child or our life partner. Next time someone tells you they love their partner, ask them what they mean by "love," and you will be surprised by how difficult it is for them to articulate it.

Indeed, as we grow out of infancy and begin to use language to express ourselves, we learn to suppress and restrict the full range of our inner experience to what can be expressed. Eventually, our imagination, our sense of wonderment and curiosity, becomes very hard to talk about, as we cannot express these concepts in words, and eventually we forget about them altogether. We become detached from unshared thoughts and yearnings, as they are submerged into the elusive depth of the unconscious mind.

This is a trap otroverts can dodge. Their strong demarcation between themselves and others allows for two separate languages: one verbal, for public interaction, and one nonverbal, or preverbal, for communicating with the self. Those who accept verbal language as the only language of the mind remember mostly through words. The otrovert remembers in feelings that cannot be articulated in words; these feelings are less likely to get lost in the recesses of memory, where they become irretrievable.

It's simple to tell a story about an experience in the physical world, which is how most people communicate efficiently. But explaining our inner world to others is not part of everyday human discourse. Since even the best spoken among us do not have the vocabulary to articulate our deepest thoughts and desires, they become literally unspeakable. Other than great artists, most of us cannot express the richness of our inner experience; when conveyed in words, most descriptions become a pale replica of the experience. Even otroverts remain limited in explaining their inner world to others, no matter how close the other person might be. This was why I could not explain to my mother why I didn't want to join the Scouts; I lacked the vocabulary to articulate why I simply did not find it attractive and to describe the inner conflict that arose in me when I heard the carefree laughter of the other boys as they boarded the buses to embark on their adventure.

Of course, the fact that others cannot access the depth of our psyche is not a bad thing in everyday life. Imagine a world in which everyone could easily read the thoughts and feelings of everyone else. We would have never been able to live together!

For the otrovert, dwelling in a rich inner world that no other human can access provides much needed solitude. It is a place where they can retreat from the chaos of the collective, a place that belongs to them and them alone. As novelist Pearl Buck once said, "Inside myself is a place where I live all alone and that is where I renew my springs that never dry up."

PART IV

THE OTROVERT LIFE

15

The Otrovert Child

As you know by now, in the first years of life, every child is an otrovert. The inner world is familiar, while the outside world is baffling and often scary. At this young age, infants spend hours floating inside their own minds; they quickly become anxious and cry in the presence of strangers and must be drawn out of themselves to engage with the communal world around them. As early as toddlerhood, they realize the perks of sacrificing their needs for the sake of group membership and plunge unquestioningly into a quest for belonging that lasts the rest of their lives. Except, of course, for otrovert children, who display some or all of the following qualities.

They have an affinity for adults over peers. Unlike shy kids, who may cling to their mothers or fathers in the presence of other grown-ups, otrovert children feel comfortable engaging with adults.

Because they spend so much time silently observing the adults around them, they are bright and funny and often say things much more mature and sophisticated than expected for their age. Though reserved around other children, they display a precocious confidence with adults and are often the darlings of shop owners, other kids' parents, teachers, and any adults who interact with them, all of whom marvel at the child's manners, thoughtfulness, and maturity. In the younger years, their social behaviors may vary, but one quality remains consistent: the otrovert child is rarely childish, even as a toddler.

They have a curious and inventive mind. In their elementary school years, otrovert children are preternaturally curious and begin to ask probing questions that challenge conventional wisdom and approach accepted knowledge from a different perspective. Among the ones I have fielded from young otroverts: "How can you do mouth-to-mouth resuscitation when we inhale oxygen and exhale carbon dioxide?" "If the fruit is alive only when connected to the tree and once picked starts dying, isn't it like us since we also start dying when disconnected from the umbilical cord?" And, perhaps most telling of all: "If you tell me not to accept anyone's ideas and to think for myself, can I also ignore that advice?" These are the hallmarks of a person who will continue to question things that most people blindly accept for as long as they live.

In later childhood, as education becomes more formalized, the desire to do well in school often comes into conflict with the otroverts' need to think for themselves. The educational system is, after all, based on communal notions, and otrovert children may experience an inner rebellion as they struggle to understand why they are expected to adhere to rules that do not make sense to them. Being specialists rather than generalists, otrovert children are idiosyncratic learners who can get lost in their own minds. The more interested they are in a subject, the more deeply they delve into it, even if it comes at the expense of focusing on what is at hand. They tend, therefore, to appear disorganized or bad at time management, spending a lot of time on some homework assignments while ignoring or putting off others. Irrespective of their intelligence level, they rarely get straight As the way that bright communal children do; rather than getting perfect scores on all subjects, otroverts excel at what they have an interest in.

In my social survival skills program for otrovert kids who have difficulties getting organized, I urge parents to watch for the line between supporting their children's independent thinking and inner defiance of authority and enabling an outward defiance of authority. In other words, if a child's otrovert traits are only theoretically disruptive to their schooling, let them be. But if a child's otrovert traits begin to have practical ramifications that prevent them from reaching their full potential—such as behavioral problems or academic performance so poor as to prevent them from advancing to the next grade—it may be necessary to step in. In general, however, otrovert kids are attentive and well behaved. While they might hold strong opinions and be stubborn and willful in a way unusual for their age, they quickly learn to mask their defiance once they realize that their rebellion is futile as long as adults are in charge.

While otroverts are not necessarily the best students, their intellect is apparent to peers and teachers alike. Moreover, the same qualities that may be disadvantageous in the context of formalized schooling will prove to be great advantages once these children graduate into the real world.

They are socially popular, but with only a few close friends or confidants. Before the age of six, it is hard to distinguish otrovert children from their communal peers. They may be more prone to daydreaming, tend not to initiate activities but rather tag along, and perhaps be a bit physically awkward. But because otrovert children are friendly, their non-belonging is not necessarily obvious to other kids. Sometimes, the otrovert child's emotional aloofness in group settings is baffling to the rest, who will make extra attempts to invite their reluctant peer into the fold. The child may tearfully beg a parent to stay when being dropped off at kindergarten or day care and typically need much encouragement to join in and play with other kids on the playground, but these behaviors are often misattributed to social anxiety or shyness, which is not uncommon in children attending school for the first time.

As they get older, otroverts' indifference to social hierarchies and disinterest in the popularity contests and cliquishness that occur within friendship groups make them a bit of an enigma to their peers. But while the distance they put between themselves and the collectives makes them hard to know, it also prevents them from being bullied or ganged up on; wielding exclusion as a form of control or punishment doesn't work on otroverts, as they were never members of the group to begin with. Despite their aversion to joining, the humor, intelligence, and gentle demeanor otrovert children typically display make them respected, well liked, and generally understood to be good company.

They are happiest when left to their own devices. That a child can contentedly play alone or together with one other child for hours and needs plenty of downtime after playing in a group tends to be the first inkling of the emerging otrovert personality. Their personal time is vital for them—something that well-meaning adults and peers often cannot understand or respect—and how they manage that time is one of the prominent traits separating otroverts from communal peers. Otrovert children are never bored in their own company but can get very bored surrounded by others, which is the opposite of how most communal people experience downtime. The difference, while lifelong, is more obvious in childhood, a period when the desire to engage in group play is thought to be an essential feature of "normal" social and emotional development.

They do not want to attend any organized activity. As otrovert children get older, they start refusing to go to after-school clubs, summer camps, class trips (especially overnight trips), and even birthday parties—any activity that does not allow some respite from the other kids. The feeling of being "trapped" with other kids is very difficult for the otrovert child. In the second decade of life, communal children will relish group bonding activities; belonging to a social group comprised of other children ("us") is a way of establishing their independence from the adults in their lives ("them"). Because the feeling of belonging is not available to the otrovert, such bonding activities can be a source of discomfort. On the other hand, otroverts don't experience the sting of rejection or exclusion the way communal children do.

They are unusually considerate and generous. The intense sensitivity to one-on-one interactions allows the otrovert to empathize with another person in a way that rarely happens in casual encounters with strangers. Whereas communal children have been socialized to see friendship as a kind of transaction in which personal sacrifices are rewarded with social inclusion, the otrovert child does not engage in the common social barter of sacrificing individual needs for communal approval and would therefore consider another's needs without feeling they deserve anything in return.

They are careful and risk averse. One otrovert I know recalls how, when she and her sister were children, their parents would often chastise her non-otrovert sibling for succumbing to peer pressure by asking, "If so-and-so jumped off a bridge, would you do it too?" The otrovert child would not jump off a bridge just because the other kids were jumping. Because otrovert children are largely immune to peer pressure, they do not engage in the kind of risky, reckless, or mischievous behavior that communal children do. Unconsumed by worries about fitting in, they have the mental space to consider the consequences of their actions and therefore are not physically adventurous, do not engage in rough-and-tumble play, and are careful not to get into trouble.

They do not deal well with change. School offers children shared but supervised time together: the perfect setting for teaching the unwritten rules of functioning in a collective. Most children learn these rules quickly and effortlessly and can swiftly adjust their behavior when new rules are introduced and old ones are replaced. But because otrovert children don't have access to the Bluetooth connection by which these implicit rules are conveyed, the otrovert cannot adapt as quickly to this sort of change. This is why disruptions both in their family, such as parents divorcing or the birth of a child, and in their schooling, such as moving to a new school, or even starting a new school year with new teachers and classmates, can be deeply disorienting for young otroverts. On the other hand, the otrovert child is a creature of habit who can easily adhere to set routines and rules as long as they meet the logic standard in the otrovert's mind.

PARENTING AN OTROVERT CHILD

Parenting an otrovert can be a baffling endeavor. The first two years of life are blissfully reassuring as the child develops much like their peers; all the standard parenting advice is pertinent, and conversations with other parents sound familiar. After this, the otrovert child starts veering into unusual territory. From then on, almost every parenting experience is unlike most other people's, leaving parents increasingly without any point of reference other than their own notions of what is expected. Behaviors that are not considered sufficiently "social" quickly become a constant source of confusion and concern for the parents, who have themselves been conditioned to view group membership as the foundation of a successful life.

This is the moment at which parents of otroverts make a decision: do we accept our child as they are, or do we endeavor to mold our child into the norm? Understandably, given that most people rely on group norms for navigating life, most parents push their children to be more sociable. Sitting alone and thinking is interpreted as frivolous "daydreaming" and discouraged. The need for privacy becomes "voluntary isolation," often prompting calls from teachers or school counselors or even visits to a therapist. Even the traits society considers unambiguously positive—intellectual curiosity, the capacity for deep perception of the world—are viewed as less important than active social-seeking behavior.

Naturally, parents are concerned about the social prospects of their children. Yet efforts to "fix" an otrovert child are certain to backfire, despite the parents' best intentions. Pushing a reluctant child into the communal version of "normalcy" makes them feel all the more abnormal. It amounts to the parents (and everyone else) telling the otrovert child that there is only one way to be. This message—that the collective confers identity and that there is only "one kind of normal"—creates an impossible dilemma for the otrovert child. They have no reason to doubt the adults who tell them—implicitly or explicitly—that wanting to belong to a group is "normal"; indeed, everyone around them behaves according to this principle. Yet it does not comport with their inner experience.

To ease their parents' distress, the otrovert child will try to fake it. They will try to enjoy what their peers enjoy and sacrifice their alone time to prove they are capable of togetherness, but in most cases, their attempts to be like the rest will make their sense of otherness even more glaring, if only to themselves.

Otrovert children who succeed in masking their differences are rewarded with popularity: a universally desired social achievement for communal children and teenagers. But popularity and the social obligations that accompany it are suffocating when one prefers solitude.

Goading otrovert children to be socially involved causes them to fight against their instincts and over time can lead to anxiety and depression. This, in turn, causes parents to become even more concerned, often misattributing their distress to loneliness, and a vicious cycle ensues.

Once otroversion is identified, parents should exercise "the art of letting be." They should recognize that time not spent socializing with a peer group is usually well spent on introspection, exploration, and personal development, and that engaging with one's inner world is no less rich or rewarding an experience than engaging with the communal one. The otrovert child's needs may be different from the majority's preferences. But they are not wrong; they are just different. And parents should recognize that forcing their otrovert child into communal experiences, like clubs and summer camps, serves only to assuage their own anxiety at the expense of their child's emotional well-being.

Giving up certain control is perhaps the greatest challenge for parents of any child or teenager. Parents feel protective of their offspring, and all children need a level of protective supervision in order to identify and avoid risk. Parents also assume that, by virtue of their more developed brains and decades of life experience, they know what is best for their still relatively unformed children. So, when it comes to social involvement, it is understandably difficult for parents to accept that their child knows who they are and what is good for them. Yet, otroverts are instinctively aware of their otherness, even if they are too young to articulate it.

Remember that these traits are innate. Forcing the otrovert child to join is therefore not going to make them a joiner. It will only cause them unnecessary emotional distress and unnecessary anxiety, while severely straining the parent-child relationship. Instead, parents should seek to understand and embrace the essence of non-belonging and try to engage their child in activities that the child finds pleasant and constructive.

One patient of mine who initially was very concerned about her otrovert child came to understand his needs so well after our conversations that she completely changed her approach to his social life—to the point where she could sometimes even see what he needed more clearly than he could. For example, when he turned five, he was of course very excited about his birthday and wanted to celebrate, as he had learned from his communal peers that birthdays are exciting and meant to be celebrated. However, she knew he would be miserable if she threw him a birthday party, even though he was too young to be able to anticipate this being the case. Instead, she took him and two other children to the movies—a structured activity where they got to sit in the dark and each choose their own candy. He loved it and was spared the inevitable disappointment and confusion of being unable to enjoy a milestone he had been so excited to celebrate.

Here are a few principles that parents can use to practice the art of letting their otrovert child be:

- **Observe and identify what your child is (and isn't) comfortable with socially.** Pressuring otrovert children into social situations that distress them—under the assumption that they have to try it and then will "learn to like it"—is unhelpful. Instead, find out what makes them feel good and what doesn't, and use it as a template for parenting. That is not to say that parents need to always acquiesce to their child's preferences, but rather that those preferences should be known and always be considered.
- **Encourage one-on-one friendships.** For most children, friendship groups offer a sense of safety, belonging, and support. When socializing with these groups, most children switch to a unified state of mind where the boundaries between the self and the collective are blurred. But otrovert children are not able to see themselves or others as anything other than discrete individuals, detached from the collective. This is why they prefer one-on-one friendships and find group activities both lonely and boring, even when the group is engaging in activities that they would otherwise enjoy. Rather than forcing otrovert children to play or socialize in large groups in the hope that friendships will develop, parents should encourage and provide

opportunities for their child to forge friendships with just one or two peers at a time.

- **Learn to enjoy their special traits.** What parent wouldn't want their child to be responsible, risk averse, and emotionally self-reliant? Remember that because otrovert children are not susceptible to peer pressure, they are reticent to engage in childhood mischief and can be trusted to avoid the risky behaviors most children try, even when unsupervised. It's tempting for a parent to let those beneficial traits be dwarfed by concerns about their child spending time alone. In a strange (but very typical) twist, these parents find themselves urging the child to be more adventurous and to take more risks. Instead, focus on the upside.

- **Trust their instincts.** Even at a very young age, otrovert children know what they want. Because they know themselves, they often choose the best course for themselves. It is often counterintuitive to trust the instincts and wishes of a young child, and obviously, parents need not simply indulge all their child's likes or dislikes. But it is also important to remember that an otrovert child can be trusted to act in their own best interest, even if they are reluctant to consult their parents or ask for their advice. When parents of otroverts think back on their child's early years, they often realize that their child knew instinctively what they needed and what was good for them. Let them follow these instincts—within reason, of course—even when most other kids move in a different direction.

- **Help them create special memories.** Otrovert children do not form shared memories. A class trip, for example, is remembered from the singular point of view. Without collective memory to lean on, otroverts are the sole custodian of their recollections. Later on in life, when they become aware of that trait, they will become more intentional about what kind of memories they make for themselves, but until then parents can play a role in helping them make everyday life worthy of remembering. When my children were younger, any time I saw something interesting or beautiful on our walks together, I would remind them to pay attention, as they were "working on creating their childhood memories." This advice doesn't apply to just otrovert children. Many children forget so many special moments of their childhood because children do not yet know to look at the world as a source of future memories. So, it is often up to the parent to help their child curate what will later become cherished memories.

Early detection of otrovert tendencies can be highly beneficial to children, making it easier for them to sort themselves out ahead of the crushing wave of adolescence, which is vital to crossing the difficult teenage years unscathed. All that is needed is an awareness of otroversion and a willingness to embrace its traits in a unique child.

16

Running the Gauntlet
of Adolescence

There is no more challenging time for otroverts than adolescence, a period when every teenager around them, regardless of social position, is vying for membership in a peer group. In a way, an adolescent group is a cult, closed off to nonmembers and ruled by the collective ethos, which requires unbridled fealty.

For communal people, adolescence is a time for figuring out what type of person they are becoming; it's the period when, aided by a newfound sense of independence, they begin to separate their personalities, values, and preferences from those of their parents.

Paradoxically, the social sorting that occurs during this period ends up becoming the primary mechanism through which the teenager's nascent sense of self develops. The sense of us versus them becomes part of the teenager's identity, along with whatever image the group chooses to project, whatever rules the group decides to follow, and whatever ideas the group decides to believe in or care about. It is in many ways a grand rehearsal for adulthood, where most people identify strongly with the groups they belong to.

Yet adolescence is unique in that these groupings are largely arbitrary, in that the group members don't really share anything other than being the same age and attending the same school. In a way, an adolescent group is a random collection of teenagers put in daily contact. Over time, friendship groups may coalesce around shared activities—the soccer players, the drama club kids, the budding musicians, and so on—but even these cliques are more a matter of proximity and convenience than true kinship. In some cases, adolescents who choose to participate in similar activities share similar curiosities or interests but are just as likely to be participating for less intrinsic reasons, such as thinking ahead to what will look good on their college applications, or because their parents enrolled them. For teenagers, the group membership itself is enough to create a sense of kinship and unite its members, whereas adults need a shared belief, interest, or cultural sameness to cohere around.

There is no question that the teenage years are the most bruising period for otroverts. For the first time, not belonging is painful. Trapped between their natural reticence and the social structures imposed on them, otroverts discover that being themselves *and* being a teenager are fundamentally incompatible. In adolescence, the group assigns one's social position, whether one likes it or not; never before or after do peers have such power over a person. Most teenagers unquestionably accept the group's rule even if it is unfavorable to them. But for otrovert teenagers, the group plays a contradictory role. On one hand, it holds no real authority; on the other, it is "the only game in town." Short, perhaps, of being homeschooled, it is virtually impossible for one to opt out. The need to fake fealty to the hive mind goes against the otrovert's instincts, and it is the first time they strongly feel their otherness since everyone around them is consumed with the endeavor of fitting in, joining, and being liked.

This pressure to mask their discomfort, combined with the teenage hormonal storm, is often what can turn meek rebels into reckless pseudo extroverts. Such a drastic behavioral reversal is not natural or comfortable to otroverts. Their inner authentic core continues to advocate meekness, even if they go to great lengths to erect a false "bad kid" facade.

In the normal order of things, teenage boys need to be loud and boisterous to be considered "socially successful," whereas social success for teenage girls depends on seeming confident. The rebellious streak in adolescence is highly valued for both genders, and the biggest risk-takers generally emerge as the natural leaders to the throng of insecure teenagers. Over time, the exhausting work of maintaining a social image based on pretense exacts a high psychological price. Being wild and boisterous is so unnatural and difficult that some otrovert teenagers start using drugs and alcohol to loosen up and make their pseudo-extrovert performance more tolerable.

Such was the case for M, a woman in her early twenties who was referred to me by her godmother, a previous patient of mine. She walked into the office almost thirty minutes late and visibly drunk, slurring her words and nearly tipping over. She sat on the couch, bleary eyed, her eye makeup smeared on her face in long black lines from crying. She said hello and then she fell asleep, slumped to the side.

M was very privileged. Her parents were rich and famous with houses and mansions all over the world, along with yachts, private planes, and memberships at exclusive private clubs, and they sent M to the best private school money could buy. But this wasn't a case of absent parents pampering their child with luxury to compensate for emotional neglect; as the only daughter in the family, she was showered with love and attention. In speaking with her family, I learned that M had been a beautiful girl who grew up to be a lovely teenager, with a fetching, self-assured demeanor that attracted romantic attention from boys and adulation from girls. She was an excellent student and liked to surf, ski, and ride horses, all of which she did with perfect ease.

Then, around the age of fourteen, she started to change. She became irritable and moody, often shouting at her parents and teachers. She started engaging in risky behaviors and became, as she described herself to me, rather harshly, "a drug addict and a whore." The change was so abrupt that she was in dire straits before anyone could come to terms with what was happening. She had an abortion, started cutting her wrists, and disappeared for days without communication, only to return drunk and inexplicably bruised. She saw some of the most renowned adolescent therapists, started on medication, and was sent to attend wilderness programs and boarding schools where it was hoped that she would build character and receive discipline, but these interventions seemed to only increase her rage, frustration, and acting out.

She received several diagnoses, including bipolar disorder and borderline personality disorder, and was treated by specialists in those fields. As soon as she became emancipated, she started splitting her time between New York and Los Angeles, where she was welcomed by the young, hip celebrity crowd. Her notoriety grew; she was known as the wildest among the wild ones. This was when I met her. At age twenty-three, she was already spent and hopeless.

After that first session when she passed out in my office, M and I connected well, and it wasn't long before her prickly and bored attitude gave way to a warm, thoughtful, and respectful one. She did not change the tenor of her behavior outside the office and continued to lead a well-publicized life of partying, debauchery, and drunkenness. But in our conversations, during which she was able to let down her carefree facade, the narrative evolving was one of sadness, emptiness, and despair. This is not unusual among some of the famous people I've worked with whose public image is very different from their private self. In my experience, however, most of these people enjoy their social position. They get their sense of self-worth from the outside, from all the adoring people around them, and so they make an effort to preserve their false persona in the public eye.

But in M's case, something was different. She disdained all the people surrounding her, and detested her notoriety. She secretly hated all those parties and preferred staying home with her dog and painting. She loved doing other things, too, but none of them seemed to comport with the way she was living her life. The only time she truly felt like herself, she told me, was when she was alone; the minute she left the house, or her posse came to her place, or a new man pursued her, she became a different person. The alcohol facilitated her wild public behavior, but ultimately, it was she who made the bad decisions.

M wasn't bipolar, suicidal, or an alcoholic; she was an otrovert. As a child, she had reigned effortlessly as the queen of the social universe, but everything changed at the onset of puberty, when her friends began to close ranks and form a cohesive, exclusive group that existed outside the attention of the adults. M was unable to truly feel part of the group, even as she was queen. What seemed exciting or important to the rest left her cold, and she could not understand why. She had every reason to be enjoying her life. Her childhood had been happy, she had every material good a person could imagine, and everyone wanted to be her friend. But despite living what many would consider a charmed life, M was deeply unhappy, and she couldn't figure out why.

Ashamed for feeling so disconnected from the group, she decided her only option was to fake it. She wanted to stay home and be alone, to disappear, rather than be popular and famous, but that seemed ungrateful. Having been given so much just for being born, she felt required to play out the role that life had seemingly cast her in. She had a friend who was very unpopular but didn't seem to care about it, and M was jealous of that ability.

Those conflicts were quickly resolved—in her mind, at least—when M discovered alcohol. When she drank, all her discomfort, inhibitions, and meekness went away. She became the rowdiest, most outrageous person in the room, which made her feel "normal," but she was not herself. She came to see that she had worn herself down trying to force herself into notoriety she did not want in the first place—that it was her circumstances that dictated she should be a social superstar, rather than her own desire. Worse, she needed alcohol to sustain the charade.

With recognition that she was an otrovert, everything clicked into place, motivating her to become sober, then to cut ties with the worst sycophants, who would drag her to parties and bring her drugs. She leaned into her love of animals and began working in animal shelters before eventually buying and moving to a farm to start an animal sanctuary.

M's story highlights one way that being a misunderstood otrovert teen can play out, particularly when the teen has been egged on by the adults and peers around them. But not all adolescent otroverts are self-destructive—at least not in the sense of engaging in risky behaviors. In fact, many have a very different experience.

In general, otroverts—both male and female—feel very conflicted about attracting attention to themselves. Risk-taking to impress the group feels silly and self-destructive, so instead of being reckless, most teenage otroverts simply attempt to blend in. But attempts at conformity—at sacrificing the self for the sake of fitting in—come no more naturally to the otrovert than does the charade of pseudo extroversion. Pretending to be interested in what they find boring and feigning excitement with the rest about things they couldn't care less about take a big toll on the otrovert. And keeping up this performance has only become more taxing in recent years, as the level of exposure and constant presence teens are expected to maintain on social media and the internet prevents the teenage otrovert from finding respite.

Today, as the mother of one twelve-year-old otrovert put it to me, her daughter cannot simply (and untruthfully) declare her love of Taylor Swift and consider the matter settled; to keep up the charade, she must quote Taylor's lyrics in her text threads and post to social media about how many hours she spent online trying to procure concert tickets. In general, the fact that adolescent life is conducted largely on public social media platforms only exacerbates teenage otroverts' vulnerability: it is the only time in their life they envy the rest and loathe how difficult it is to be themselves.

It is crucial that parents identify the otrovert trait in their teenager and make themselves aware of the challenges this entails. Telltale signs might include the following:

- Disinterest in teenage drama, popularity contents, or gossip
- Feelings of inadequacy or otherness that seem incompatible with their social status or how they appear to others
- Suddenly adopting a hyperextroverted persona (in real-life interactions and on social media) that is not their own
- Reluctance to attend parties or celebrate rites of passage such as bar and bat mitzvahs, quinceañeras, or graduations

- Dressing very differently, listening to different kinds of music, and showing interest in different kinds of activities compared with their peers
- Refusal to participate in team sports, especially if the teen showed an interest in athleticism as a child
- The desire for more alone time (even if they do not indulge that desire); socializing with friends one-on-one rather than in groups
- Pragmatism, a lack of adventurousness, and an adultlike ability to assess risk

Displaying a few of these qualities does not necessarily mean that your teenager is an otrovert. But displaying most or all of these traits is a sign that a teen may be going through life feeling like a perpetual outsider. If this is the case, it's important to approach the teenage otrovert in a way that won't trigger their inner rebellion—to think of a teenage otrovert as a teenager first and an otrovert second. Parents should avoid comments that will trigger the feelings of confusion, shame, and alienation that come from feeling misaligned with the group's trajectory, and instead point out the difference in importance that the otrovert assigns to certain aspects of teenage life relative to others. Even if their attempts at broaching a discussion are rejected at first, it's vital that parents do all they can to help their otrovert teen understand and make room for this facet of who they are.

If a teen can traverse the gauntlet of adolescence unscathed, they emerge wanting to never be anyone else. How they navigate these years can make the difference between a rich life spent engaged in what they enjoy and are good at and a life compromised by the pursuit of impossible goals and many regrets.

Extolling a life of individualism to a member of the most conformist age group can alarm them and cause retreat; eventually, however, most otrovert teens will outgrow the feelings of inadequacy and weirdness they experience in the group, freeing up mental space to understand and embrace their differences, and live life more authentically and fully.

17

Romantic Relationships

Recently, an otrovert in her late thirties whom we'll call R confided in me that she was struggling in her love life. She desperately wanted to get married and had been online dating for a number of years, wholly unsuccessfully. Then she came right out and asked me, "Will I ever be able to forge a deep romantic relationship with a communal person, or am I only ever going to be compatible with other nonjoiners like me?"

The fact that otroverts are significantly underrepresented in our pluralist society makes the possibility of meeting an otrovert partner relatively low. Since otroverts struggle with being out in public, they are most likely to meet a romantic partner by chance or online than at a party or within the walls of a crowded bar. These difficulties are only amplified by the fact that during the years when people typically become interested in courtship, most otroverts don't understand their non-belonging, feel inferior to belongers, and struggle unsuccessfully to be like the rest.

But once an otrovert emerges from the gauntlet of adolescence with a better sense of who they are, it becomes much easier to find a romantic partner who shares their view of the world—and when they do, they can quickly forge a strong bond. After all, otroverts are keen observers and empaths. Moreover, in a committed, long-term romantic relationship, it is all but impossible for the otrovert to successfully mask their non-belonging; in time, their facade will crumble, allowing them to show up authentically as who they are.

When both partners are otroverts, they respect each other's boundaries and base their relationship on mutual understanding rather than social conventions. Being highly attuned to other individuals—as well as themselves—otrovert couples are close to each other without being enmeshed. They create a covenant of mutual respect, cemented by their strong inner rebellion against social conventions. They also tend to be very loyal and protective of each other and do not feel jealous of or threatened by the other's accomplishments. As equally unconventional thinkers, they show a keen interest in others' imaginative ideas and original thoughts. That stimulates a unique dynamic in which creativity and reinvention are essential to the functioning of their unit.

Most couples are a union of two people who enter the relationship with distinct social and cultural identities that color how they understand—or more often misunderstand—each other. Think, for example, about couples in which one person is a devout

Catholic and the other is an atheist, or in which one person grew up as a member of the 1 percent while the other lived paycheck to paycheck. In communal couples, these differences are so central to the identity of each person that they can become a recurring source of conflict and complications. The otrovert couple is un-encumbered by such baggage. Even if the two come from very different religious backgrounds, social classes, ethnicities, and so forth, they feel little connection or allegiance to them. As a result, the chance of these differences causing conflict or friction is van-ishingly low.

Obviously, otrovert couples fight like every other couple and are not immune to disagreements about petty things. But when it comes to the big things—like child-rearing, family obligations, and how to manage their social lives—differences of opinion are rare, and generally a matter of degree: what is seen as a neces-sary social obligation to one may not be deemed necessary by the other, for example. Because they are outwardly accommodating by nature, they can be convinced to reconsider a strongly held posi-tion that is in direct conflict with their partner's. It is easier for an otrovert to be part of an otrovert couple for mainly one reason: it maximizes the chances that both partners innately understand what communal people cannot—what life as a non-belonger is like.

Which brings us back to the question R posed to me: can an otrovert forge a successful, lasting romantic partnership with someone who is not an otrovert? It is initially hard for belongers to understand non-belongers and vice versa, so it makes sense that having two very different ways of seeing the world could produce a variety of mutual misunderstandings. Early on in the relationship, the intense resistance to certain things most consider negotiable, disinterest in things universally considered "fun," and unshakable inner conviction (some might say stubbornness) in someone who otherwise comes across as very accommodating and considerate can be baffling to the non-otrovert partner. As the relationship develops, the otrovert's certain aloofness, resistance to traditions and social gatherings, and awkwardness in group settings can be frustrating—especially if the partner is highly social, has a huge family that loves to gather for holidays, or has a job that requires them to attend many functions they are embarrassed to always attend solo. And so most "mixed" couples—otroverts and communal people—need to work harder to be successful. But that is not at all a bad thing!

Incompatibilities of all kinds pose great opportunities for all couples to learn about each other; while they may have to invest more effort into seeking compromises and understanding, this investment pays dividends in the form of more intimate, deeper bonds. Beyond the initial "getting to know you" period, most communal couples invest very little time or effort in deepening their understanding of each other, assuming that at some point over the course of their lives together, they will be able to find common ground. When you stop to think about it, the idea of living with someone you met as a stranger for the rest of your life is mind-bogglingly odd. Nothing prepares us for it, and the notion that any two people will view the world through identical lenses is an insult to everything we know about human consciousness.

Yet most people don't listen to each other with deep interest and empathy, and genuine attempts to see things from a partner's perspective are rare and unexpected.

This is where the mixed otrovert and communal couple shines. The differences between a communal person and an otrovert are more apparent and show up earlier than other differences between romantic partners. Again, this friction is a good thing: it allows the couple to consider their differences early on. Meanwhile, having a partner who is willing and able to take on the lion's share of the small talk at unavoidable communal gatherings, or who has a large circle of friends to go out with, leaving the other person to enjoy their alone time, can be a huge source of relief for the otrovert—and these things are rarely a source of conflict when expectations are set near the start.

No matter how hard they try, otrovert partners especially are unlikely to learn to love (or even get used to) some communal aspects of life with the passage of time. Being an otrovert is not something we grow out of—nor should we want it to be. Once a communal partner can understand the salient aspects of the non-belonger, they can share in closeness without codependency. Gaining empathy without judgment of each other's needs paves the way to any number of solutions.

For example, an otrovert married to a social person understands that their spouse has the need to go to parties or other social events like group trips, while they feel perfectly content to be excluded from their partner's rich social life. And so it is quite easy to come to a mutual understanding that the social spouse will do these things alone, with no resentment on either side. Or, if one person in the relationship likes to do dinners with other couples, they can limit it to one other couple at a time rather than many.

One otrovert described to me how, when she and her husband go out with friends, there's always a predetermined exit time and strategy, with an excuse queued up in case the friends want to extend the evening. Knowing that there's an agreed-upon departure time alleviates her anxiety about the evening stretching on for longer than she can bear and allows him to enjoy the company of friends without having to worry that she has exceeded her threshold and is silently desperate to leave. When a sacrifice is unavoidable, the mutual understanding that neither partner's preference is any more or less justified allows the couple to reach a fair compromise.

Otroverts also bring something extra to relationships. Here are a few benefits of pairing off romantically with an otrovert.

They put their partner first. The hive views any couple as one node in its social network, which also includes family, friends, neighbors, and coworkers, who are often considered legitimate competitors for a couple's attention to each other. Otroverts don't prioritize the collective this way. They are very present for their significant other and deeply invested in family life, which they prioritize over their careers and other socially sanctioned notions of success.

They have an innate capacity for intimacy. Throughout our lives, we receive implicit instructions and training on how to behave within the collective, but no one tells us how to live as a couple. The social skills a communal person possesses aren't the same as the skills needed for a successful intimate relationship, and vice versa. Whatever an otrovert may lack in the social skills department, they compensate for by being highly skilled in fostering intimacy.

They don't try to fit the relationship into the communal mold. Otroverts understand that what is good for one relationship will not necessary be good for another; in fact, attempts to model one's relationship on that of another couple or on what society tells us healthy relationships should look like is a big reason so many marriages are unhappy. The otrovert's ability to know what feels right without looking to others for guidance is invaluable in all relationships, romantic or otherwise.

In short, otroverts like R should not despair. As an otrovert, you do not need to be understood so much as accepted by your partner in order to create a wonderful, complementary, and long-lasting bond.

18

Otroverts at Work

In adulthood, the otrovert can choose how to run their life, especially in terms of which relationships to cultivate (or not) and
how they spend their leisure time. But while it may be relatively
easy to opt out of relationships or activities that do not serve
them, the one aspect of communal life that most otroverts (and
other healthy adults) cannot avoid is work. The fact that many
jobs require some degree of collaboration, consensus, and partici-
pation in communal rituals—from attending office holiday parties
to navigating the politics of small talk—means that work is often
the biggest challenge to the otrovert's silent rebelliousness. But it
doesn't have to be, as long as the otrovert has stopped to carefully
consider what kind of work environment they need and what they
are good at.

The environments that most people seem to tolerate—or

even thrive in—are impossible for otroverts. Professions that allow work to be done collaboratively—such as pilot, teacher, or researcher—are so taxing for the otrovert that very little energy is left for actually doing the work. Whereas teamwork, togetherness, and collaboration are stressful, a profession that allows one to work independently—as a consultant, a writer, a photographer, a solopreneur, or an independent contractor, for example—will likely be a good match for the otrovert. It does not have to be a high-powered or prestigious job so long as there is an opportunity for self-generated decisions and the freedom to come up with ideas that do not conform to the consensus.

My patient D was a human resources manager in a big company when she came to see me in desperation. She was very talented and successful but kept changing jobs frequently. The pattern was always the same. She'd start a new job with great energy, brimming with ideas, connecting easily with her coworkers, and feeling that she'd found, at last, the place where she could settle down. Sooner or later, however, she started experiencing a growing emotional fatigue, followed by depression and overwhelm so severe that she struggled to attend even the most routine meetings. She dreaded Mondays with every fiber of her being, spent her days counting the hours until the workday was over, and dragged herself home feeling exhausted and dispirited. Though it had happened several times, she could never explain this trajectory, not even to herself. Nothing happened at work to make her feel this way, but she felt distinctly that work was the sole reason for her darkening mood.

She visited me after trying a number of therapies and determining that none had helped. "Perhaps the workplace, not what happens there, brings you down," I suggested. She didn't see how this illuminated her situation. "Or," I ventured, "maybe it's not the kind of work for you." She was still not impressed with my input. This was the work she'd done all her life and where her expertise lay, she told me. "Plus," she said, "I actually love HR."

I suspected that she needed to find a way to apply all that talent and expertise in a different kind of environment. We explored her experiences with different work environments and quickly discovered that she was much better at doing special assignments than at "keeping the trains running on time." Routine meetings, conferences, and roundtable seminars all felt exhausting and grueling to her—and she believed them to be a giant waste of time. Since her work had always been a daily amalgamation of individual projects and all forms of meetings, she realized that she was becoming worn out from only certain aspects of the work.

Over time, she realized that if she stayed in the corporate world, she would not be able to find a job that allowed her to focus exclusively on the kind of independent and self-directed work that energized her. She was a soloist who simply could not play in an orchestra. So she decided to open her own HR consulting agency, which supported her need for independence; she would be her own boss, which would allow her to spend her working hours doing only the things she liked to do. Eight years later, her agency is thriving, her talents are much better utilized, and most importantly, she actually looks forward to every Monday.

D's example illustrates why otroverts are not successful within rigid institutions where they are unable to be in control of how they spend their time. And her experience is not at all unusual. Many otroverts I have counseled have described being unable to function under similar circumstances; they cannot lie low, play nice, and toe the line, however they may try. The fact is, the otrovert personality is incompatible with many features of corporate life: from being forced to waste hours a day in pointless meetings, to having projects stalled by red tape and bureaucracy, to the exhausting task of navigating all the power grabbing and status seeking (aka "office politics"). Worse yet is having to watch their opinions and ideas be brushed aside in favor of the group consensus, all while working in an environment where they are being constantly distracted by colleagues, clients, and an ever-expanding inbox.

This is all exceedingly tiresome to otroverts, who sooner or later will discover that they do their best work on their own, in environments where they can make their own decisions and are solely accountable for the successes and the failures. With no one to ask, no one to consult, and no one to share the responsibility with—a terrifying prospect for communal people—otroverts are free to do what they do best: think creatively and expansively, outside the hive.

Choosing the right job or career is hugely important for everyone, but this is especially true for otroverts. One reason is that otroverts do not compartmentalize their lives, with one part dedicated to work, one part dedicated to leisure, one to family, and so on. Their inner world—which is obviously present wherever they are—is the epicenter of their lives. It is therefore impossible to thrive in a work environment that is incompatible with their inner lives.

When situated within their comfort zone, otroverts can be extremely productive and successful, even if that success may not be obvious. Albert Einstein, perhaps the most famous otrovert, was considered mentally handicapped in childhood and was a high school dropout. He conceived of relativity in his early twenties while working as a clerk in the Swiss government patent office, which gave him time and space to think alone at his desk while still providing enough structure to his days to prevent him from drifting.

Because otroverts strive to adapt their work life to their abilities and inabilities rather than try to change themselves to meet the demands of a job, accurately identifying their comfort zone is the key to professional success for otroverts. Other ingredients for professional success include the following:

- A profession where nonconventional thinking is essential for success.
- A balance between exposure to others and being alone. It cannot be an entirely solitary profession, but on the other hand, it cannot be a profession with constant unmitigated contact with others. The presence of others, even without interaction (such as an open workspace or open-door policy), is very distracting to otroverts, who lack the ability to be "always on."

- A profession where the otrovert has a clearly defined role that sets them apart from the rest of the group (similar to the way a role helps them in social situations).
- Self-employment, or a profession that can eventually provide a path to self-employment, such as working as a consultant or a freelancer or owning one's own business, as long as the day-to-day work doesn't involve cold calls, solicitation, or dependency on many suppliers that must be interacted with regularly.
- A leadership role. Otroverts are natural-born leaders. Inwardly defiant in the face of authority, they would rather tell others what to do than be subject to the rules, regulations, and whims of others.
- A job that leaves time for creative pursuits and is also itself at least partially a creative pursuit.
- A rhythm that creates a predictable routine—not much travel, and not many meetings or conventions outside the workplace.

Whereas communal people can handle soul-crushing drudgery, the otrovert cannot ignore a lack of job satisfaction. Otroverts cannot barter with themselves, as in "My work gives me no space for individual thinking but compensates by offering long weekends and many vacation days." This is related to otroverts' unusual perception of the passage of time. No minute can be sacrificed. No phase of the day or of the year or of life is redundant. Every minute of life is important and cannot be "saved for the future."

In a way, succeeding as an otrovert in a world of joiners is dependent on remaining an outsider in the workplace. Unlike many communal people, otroverts don't consider their profession or job title to be a central part of their identity; they define themselves by who they are rather than what they do and feel no particular sense of connection or loyalty to the organization where they are employed.

Even the concept of success for otroverts is a personal rather than relational concept; psychologically, whether the team succeeds or fails is less important than the otrovert's own performance. Success is not predicated on winning, being recognized, making a lot of money, or being promoted, valuations that are etched into the DNA of joiners. Whether the group considers an otrovert successful is irrelevant—otroverts achieve professional fulfillment by tapping into their strengths, and doing good work is much more satisfying when the others have no power to grade their success.

Most people who want to become prima ballerinas are still content to stay with the troupe as part of the ensemble—some may ultimately discover they prefer to be in the second tier. But not otroverts: they are soloists by temperament.

19

Old Age and Death

What does it actually mean to belong? I would argue that belonging is a fiction, a concept that exists only in our minds. In a way, nothing belongs to us, and we don't belong to anything. Even our most personal property, our body, is only ours to use for at most eight or nine decades, and our control of its fate is limited at best. Just as possessions can be taken away, destroyed, or lost, so can friendships, camaraderie, and relationships we consider "ours." The illusion of ownership over our social relationships is up there with the illusion of immortality and permanence.

We can, however, own our memories. Otroverts know this instinctively, and it allows them to build rich, meaningful lives made up of unique moments and experiences, all the way to the end.

For most otroverts, the last decades of life are a time of peace and contentment. Save for debilitating conditions, they arrive at the final phase of earthly life rather cheerfully. They have curated life around their needs, cultivated a rich inner world, and invested in creating pleasant memories, which are the only assets that truly belong to each of us. They understand, at least on some level, that our experiences are etched in our memory regardless of whether we want to remember them or not. The protected storage of the mind makes every investment in memories a secure deposit: no one can take it away from us.

Once most of life is in the rearview mirror and memories come to occupy larger and larger swaths of the psyche, this investment pays great dividends.

Communal people feel the urgent slippage of life as they age. Having lived their lives under communal dictates, many are saddled with regrets—"What was I thinking? How did I let myself...?" The reality that the exit from this world, much like the entry, is a solitary, lonely experience is terrifying for communal people. With less future to plan for and painful memories haunting them, their later years may be marred by distress. The barter they so willingly engaged in for so long—the shared life in exchange for an examined one—starts losing its buoyancy as they approach old age.

After a lifetime of choices dictated by group norms, communal people finally realize that the group cannot teach each member how to die alone. Many find it quite difficult to communicate with a dying loved one, and no one can truly ever know what that person is going through. It's as though the dying person is suddenly totally alone on a journey that no one can join even if they want to. The terror of having to face death alone, the realization that togetherness was only an illusion, becomes increasingly intolerable, as communal people become lonely and isolated exactly when they need others most. This is one of the paradoxes of human existence: at the end of life, when facing what is arguably the loneliest struggle a person can experience, suddenly all the years spent devoted to the group evaporate. Aligning with a collective can be a salve, or at least a distraction, in the face of this existential dread. As David Foster Wallace observes in his famous essay "A Supposedly Fun Thing I'll Never Do Again,"[3] which describes a cruise vacation he took through the characteristically otrovert lens of a detached observer, "A vacation is a respite from unpleasantness, and since consciousness of death and decay are unpleasant, it may seem weird that Americans' ultimate fantasy vacation involves being plunked down in an enormous primordial engine of death and decay. But on a 7NC Luxury Cruise, we are skillfully enabled in the construction of various fantasies of triumph over just this death and decay.... The 7NC's constant activities, parties, festivities, gaiety and song; the adrenaline, the excitement, the stimulation. It makes you feel vibrant, alive.... [This] option promises not a transcendence of death-dread so much as just drowning it out."

For otroverts, their whole lives have, in a sense, been a solitary

---

3   David Foster Wallace, "A Supposedly Fun Thing I'll Never Do Again," *A Supposedly Fun Thing I'll Never Do Again* (New York: Little, Brown, 1997).

journey, so as the final exit beckons on the horizon, they are less likely to fear dying alone. The French philosopher and author Albert Camus wrote of how, in the face of existential dread, we can commit philosophical suicide and join a group that reassures us of an afterlife, or accept our fate as entirely our own. Otroverts see their fate as theirs, and theirs alone. Being unbound by any religion, the otrovert is not subscribed to a preordained belief system regarding what happens after death. Instead, the otrovert can create their own narrative about their own fate. Whether this narrative is "correct" is of no consequence; they are firm in their convictions because those convictions are theirs and theirs alone.

When I started treating U, she was ninety-three and I was forty-three. At this point in my life, I could not fathom how the end of life would feel, but we often talked about death in our sessions—not because she had fears she needed to work through but because "at this stage," she would say, chuckling, "death is the primary plan for the future." U was an esteemed academic, a professor emerita at a prestigious university who led a bohemian life in the East Village—a heavy smoker in Levi's. Even in her tenth decade of life, she was spunky, opinionated, and self-reliant; based on these and several other qualities, I suspected she had been a lifelong otrovert. She told me that when she learned about the concept of death as a child, she was very scared. Not about her own death but about the future death of her parents and having to continue without them. Now that it was the other way around— she would be leaving people behind to continue without her—she was not afraid. She saw no reason to be.

Many old people are so miserable at the end of life that they beg for death, even as they fear it. But U was different. "I still enjoy most of what I always have," she told me. "Rosemary and lavender, good weed, coffee, looking at the sunset, and walking. I've always lived my life for myself," she continued. "Now I will die for myself without regrets."

It is no coincidence that in a communal society such as ours, so many religious traditions believe that our souls live on in some form, released from the tethers of our physical body, after we die. Those who have lived their lives among others want to return to earth, where they can be with others, or end up in the afterlife with their deceased family members. But even among those who hold these beliefs, the uncertainty—the not knowing for sure—is what frightens them the most. This was not the case for U. "Death makes sense to me," she explained. "It always made sense, and I have arrived at this juncture as prepared as I can be. I lived my personal life, of which I am proud, between me and myself, and I will die my personal death."

U died a few years later in her sleep, of old age. She was ninety-eight and had lived her life to the fullest. She owed nothing to anyone and felt no one owed her anything either. She had spent her life caring for others not out of social obligation or duty but out of empathy. Even at the very end, she was not fearful or bitter or nostalgic. I am not sure what she learned from me, but I know what I learned from her: finding peace in your life makes it easier to feel at peace in death. And to find peace in your life, you must first learn to be at peace with yourself, which includes understanding and embracing the ways that you are different from everyone else.

The fact that each one of us has one life, and that we each have a responsibility to make the most of it, is universally understood but rarely acted on. In some cases, that's because we aren't sufficiently in touch with ourselves to know what it means to make the most of our limited time. In other cases, we might fear this attitude will be viewed as self-centered because it requires prioritizing your individual needs over the collective's rather than ignoring the inner voice that urges you to do something for yourself. At almost every juncture in our lives, the choice appears binary: you can either sacrifice your needs for those of your group or act upon your urges with no regard for the rest.

If you are lucky enough to arrive at old age, the fallacy of that choice is eventually laid bare. You realize that the battle between two opposing interests—yours versus the group's—was never a fair fight. As death approaches, the group doesn't stop or slow down for you, which means you have to learn to get along with yourself, because as the camaraderie and the togetherness slowly fade away, you are all that you have.

Otroverts have always known this. They have learned over their lifetimes that taking care of themselves is not mutually exclusive with being generous and considerate to others: you can remain loyal to yourself while negotiating amicably with the rest. You can decide to like yourself, or at least accept yourself. After all, there is great peace in knowing that your mind is the only thing you will ever truly own, that it cannot be taken from you, and that it will be with you unconditionally as you grow old and face the end.

As Emily Dickinson wrote,

There is a solitude of space
A solitude of sea
A solitude of death, but these
Society shall be
Compared with that profounder site
That polar privacy
A soul admitted to itself—
Finite infinity.

Conclusion

O troverts are all around us. They have always been, even if we haven't had a name for them until now. If, like me, you are one of them, I hope you have recognized yourself in these pages. Whether you are an otrovert or not, I hope you will come away from this book with a greater appreciation for the virtues of the otrovert personality, and what we all can learn from them.

In recent years, there has been much hand-wringing over the record levels of loneliness, alienation, and polarization that plague our society today. Countless writers, thinkers, policymakers, and even the US surgeon general have cited the decline of communal life as a principal cause of this mental health epidemic and proposed a variety of communal solutions ranging from getting off social media and expanding our social support networks to getting more involved in our local communities and so forth. In theory, these ideas are not without merit. But in practice, we are a society having more and more conversations about the importance of community while continuing to become lonelier and more divided than ever. Otroverts are well equipped not only to thrive in our fractured, angry world, but also to show others the way. The reason for this is simple: they know how to forge deep and fulfilling relationships with themselves.

Emotional self-sufficiency is a precondition for both happiness and success, not just for them but for everyone. To be a valuable member of a group, a team, or a community, you must have a good relationship with yourself too. Despite their proclivity to focus on themselves rather than the collective, otroverts don't eschew social connection. They simply see people, *including* themselves, as individuals, not just faceless members of a group. It is easy to hate a formless group that you are taught to perceive as different, inferior, or threatening. But it is much harder to generalize your hostility when you grasp people as individuals. Otroverts show us that it does not need to be so hard to be genuinely caring about the plight of another. In dismantling reductive notions of "us versus them," they demonstrate how to exercise empathy, bridge tribal differences, and get along with people better.

So many of my patients come to see me because they are feeling weighed down by unnecessary burdens they put on their lives, for reasons they can't understand. Their loads invariably become lighter once they realize that they do not need anyone's approval for any choice they make in life. Otroverts understand this instinctively. But for communal people, it is a corrective emotional experience. Because once we learn to distinguish between our own needs and those of the group, then decide for ourselves which ones really matter, our lives become infinitely easier. We begin to think of ourselves as the lead character in our own lives rather than the extra. We can liberate ourselves from the hive mind and begin to see the world from a clearer, unobstructed perspective. Favoring the group's interests over our own is perhaps good for getting along with others, but it is not suitable for getting along with ourselves.

Otroverts are self-interested, but they are not competitive. Unfortunately, success in a communal environment is based on competition, which is often unfair and tinged with aggression. Because groups, especially in the professional world, are ruled by those who adhere to this way of being, our performance is being judged by those who are marked to succeed in this way. Those who shy away from confrontation, who would prefer not to be perceived as mean, and who are inclined to give rather than take are unlikely to succeed in competition against those who are less thoughtful and more brazen. To even the playing field, we teach them to conform to the predominant behavior: to be assertive, speak up, and stop being people pleasers. In so doing, we reinforce the toxic notion that being kind and self-effacing is a weakness.

Otroverts have much to teach these people about how to suc-ceed in a gentler, more benevolent way. They refuse to blindly follow the rules of aggression that they have neither initiated nor fully understand. They define success by what one achieves, not by what one achieves in relation to others. And their consideration of others stems from their natural empathy rather than because they have been taught to "be kind to others." Their lesson, and it is one I deeply believe, is that the best things in life are cruelty free.

There is always a choice to be either helpful or hostile, and so many choose the latter, for no discernable reason.

Otroverts don't have this choice; they are compelled to be considerate. No matter how many people are present, otroverts see each one separately. In theory, humanity extols benevolence. However, in practice, competitiveness, confrontation, and discrimination are much more common than acceptance or kindness.

At best, our society regards benevolence as a form of social capital and not a goal in and of itself. This is surprising, considering that the experience of being kind is so rewarding to you and everyone around you. We should be very eager to be kind, but the reality is that while kindness is commendable, humans respect power more. And power is something humans are disinclined to share. In virtually every field, the most powerful positions are reached by knocking others down along the way. This creates a vicious cycle by which the more power one accumulates, the more selfishly and competitively one behaves. The truly altruistic among us may win our admiration but rarely achieve money, power, and the other trappings of human success.

Being considerate because of empathy rather than training is not only more rewarding, it also makes the lives of those around us more pleasant. It is a win-win situation. Just imagine a world where everyone is gentle and considerate. Where everyone is free to live a quiet life, free of conflict and malice. A place where there is no social penalty for refusing to bully one's way to success. This may sound like a utopia, but I believe it can be a reality if the lessons of the otrovert life are shared widely.

As a child, I read and reread a beautiful story called *King Matt the First*,[4] about a child prince who becomes a king following his father's death. He is trying to create just laws to benefit children, but his best intentions are thwarted by the adults acting in their own selfish interests. It was written by Janusz Korczak, a Polish pediatrician who founded and ran a Jewish orphanage in Warsaw. When the Nazis conquered Poland and came for the orphans, Dr. Korczak made the choice to die with them. Does it matter that his death was noble? I would argue not only that it does, but that the footprint of his benevolence continues to exist. To me, Dr. Korczak is a giant even if no one remembers him or *King Matt the First*.

A benevolent footprint is not difficult to attain; all you need to do is tap into your inner rebel. Instead of unconditionally endorsing the status quo, you can interrogate and challenge it. You need not be an otrovert to reject the hive-mind consensus. It is a simple matter of creating enough distance between the self and the collective.

Cruelty is far too high a price to pay for the privilege of belonging. Whether you are an otrovert or not, you need no permission to let go of the unkind, the cruel, and the selfish. At a time when the Trumpian hive mind's demands for assertiveness and aggression grow louder and more insistent than ever, it is up to all of us to choose the gentler, kinder path. As Ibsen wrote in *An Enemy of the People*, "When society's values are corrupted, it is the duty of the individual to uphold true morality."

---

4   Janusz Korczak, *King Matt the First* (Warsaw: Farrar, Straus and Giroux, 1923).

Are You an Otrovert?

Circle the number below each statement that applies to you. When you're done, add up your total points.

If you scored 188 or above, you are likely an otrovert. If so, I hope this book has helped you better understand and celebrate this unique facet of who you are.

If you scored below 188, you are likely *not* an otrovert. If this is the case, I hope this book has helped you better understand and celebrate the otroverts in your life.

	Very Strongly Agree	Strongly Agree	Agree	Neither Agree nor Disagree	Disagree	Strongly Disagree	Very Strongly Disagree
1	I feel lonely in large social gatherings.						
	7	6	5	4	3	2	1
2	I am truly close to very few people in my life.						
	7	6	5	4	3	2	1
3	I enjoy parties and party as often as possible.						
	1	2	3	4	5	6	7
4	I need a lot of time by myself.						
	7	6	5	4	3	2	1

#	Statement	Very Strongly Agree	Strongly Agree	Agree	Neither Agree nor Disagree	Disagree	Strongly Disagree	Very Strongly Disagree
5	When I am sad I need people to cheer me up.	1	2	3	4	5	6	7
6	I like being alone; I am my best company.	7	6	5	4	3	2	1
7	I am the first one to hear about hot new places.	1	2	3	4	5	6	7
8	I like to work on my own.	7	6	5	4	3	2	1

(continued)

9 I do not need others' approval for my beliefs.

Very Strongly Agree	Strongly Agree	Agree	Neither Agree nor Disagree	Disagree	Strongly Disagree	Very Strongly Disagree
7	6	5	4	3	2	1

10 I am a follower of an organized religion.

Very Strongly Agree	Strongly Agree	Agree	Neither Agree nor Disagree	Disagree	Strongly Disagree	Very Strongly Disagree
1	2	3	4	5	6	7

11 I am a heavy user of social media.

Very Strongly Agree	Strongly Agree	Agree	Neither Agree nor Disagree	Disagree	Strongly Disagree	Very Strongly Disagree
1	2	3	4	5	6	7

12 I have nothing to hide, but I prefer to keep my life to myself anyway.

Very Strongly Agree	Strongly Agree	Agree	Neither Agree nor Disagree	Disagree	Strongly Disagree	Very Strongly Disagree
7	6	5	4	3	2	1

	Very Strongly Agree	Strongly Agree	Agree	Neither Agree nor Disagree	Disagree	Strongly Disagree	Very Strongly Disagree
13	I mistrust conventional wisdom; it is groupthink.						
	7	6	5	4	3	2	1
14	I consider thinking an activity.						
	7	6	5	4	3	2	1
15	I am an observer of life, not an active participant.						
	7	6	5	4	3	2	1
16	I do not like to be alone.						
	1	2	3	4	5	6	7

(continued)

#	Statement	Very Strongly Agree	Strongly Agree	Agree	Neither Agree nor Disagree	Disagree	Strongly Disagree	Very Strongly Disagree
17	I think most people do not know that I am shy.	7	6	5	4	3	2	1
18	I like to wear bright colors; they make me to stand out in the crowd.	1	2	3	4	5	6	7
19	I like to get attention from those around me.	1	2	3	4	5	6	7
20	The opinion of others is very important to me.	1	2	3	4	5	6	7

#	Statement	Very Strongly Agree	Strongly Agree	Agree	Neither Agree nor Disagree	Disagree	Strongly Disagree	Very Strongly Disagree
21	I think sharing a working space is good for sharing ideas.	1	2	3	4	5	6	7
22	I like it when others agree with me.	1	2	3	4	5	6	7
23	I don't mind being in the minority.	7	6	5	4	3	2	1
24	I develop a personal philosophy to guide my life rather than adopting one from the outside.	7	6	5	4	3	2	1

(continued)

	Very Strongly Agree	Strongly Agree	Agree	Neither Agree nor Disagree	Disagree	Strongly Disagree	Very Strongly Disagree
25	I want to be understood.						
	1	2	3	4	5	6	7
26	I am sometimes scared by my own thoughts.						
	7	6	5	4	3	2	1
27	I own and stand behind my views.						
	7	6	5	4	3	2	1
28	I think every question has an answer.						
	1	2	3	4	5	6	7

29	I don't accept any ideas or notions without examining them myself.						
	Very Strongly Agree	Strongly Agree	Agree	Neither Agree nor Disagree	Disagree	Strongly Disagree	Very Strongly Disagree
	7	6	5	4	3	2	1

30	I have to be my own boss.						
	Very Strongly Agree	Strongly Agree	Agree	Neither Agree nor Disagree	Disagree	Strongly Disagree	Very Strongly Disagree
	7	6	5	4	3	2	1

31	I think that each problem has many possible solutions.						
	Very Strongly Agree	Strongly Agree	Agree	Neither Agree nor Disagree	Disagree	Strongly Disagree	Very Strongly Disagree
	7	6	5	4	3	2	1

32	I think my teachers or superiors are always right.						
	Very Strongly Agree	Strongly Agree	Agree	Neither Agree nor Disagree	Disagree	Strongly Disagree	Very Strongly Disagree
	1	2	3	4	5	6	7

(continued)

33 I have my best ideas in meetings.

Very Strongly Agree	Strongly Agree	Agree	Neither Agree nor Disagree	Disagree	Strongly Disagree	Very Strongly Disagree
1	2	3	4	5	6	7

34 I am naturally eclectic rather than specialized.

Very Strongly Agree	Strongly Agree	Agree	Neither Agree nor Disagree	Disagree	Strongly Disagree	Very Strongly Disagree
7	6	5	4	3	2	1

35 I rely on myself. Asking for help is difficult.

Very Strongly Agree	Strongly Agree	Agree	Neither Agree nor Disagree	Disagree	Strongly Disagree	Very Strongly Disagree
7	6	5	4	3	2	1

36 When I share stories about myself, I try to be accurate in every detail.

Very Strongly Agree	Strongly Agree	Agree	Neither Agree nor Disagree	Disagree	Strongly Disagree	Very Strongly Disagree
1	2	3	4	5	6	7

37	I believe the only wisdom is the one that is coming down the generations.						
	Very Strongly Agree	Strongly Agree	Agree	Neither Agree nor Disagree	Disagree	Strongly Disagree	Very Strongly Disagree
	1	2	3	4	5	6	7

38	I have a deep respect for authority figures.						
	Very Strongly Agree	Strongly Agree	Agree	Neither Agree nor Disagree	Disagree	Strongly Disagree	Very Strongly Disagree
	1	2	3	4	5	6	7

39	I love new ideas.						
	Very Strongly Agree	Strongly Agree	Agree	Neither Agree nor Disagree	Disagree	Strongly Disagree	Very Strongly Disagree
	7	6	5	4	3	2	1

40	I often question myself.						
	Very Strongly Agree	Strongly Agree	Agree	Neither Agree nor Disagree	Disagree	Strongly Disagree	Very Strongly Disagree
	7	6	5	4	3	2	1

Acknowledgments

This is a work of an otrovert. As such it cannot be the fruit of a team effort and presents a dearth of people to acknowledge. But those I mention here were indispensable to the making of this book. Therefore, these acknowledgments are short on collaborators but full of gratitude.

First, I want to acknowledge Maya Beiser, my life partner and the most influential person in my life. I also want to acknowledge our children, Aurielle and Dorian. Living with my little family in peace and harmony has been a great privilege and pleasure. They have allowed me to find refuge from the world churning outside and given me a reason and a way to belong.

My work on non-belonging extended for many years, solitary but not isolated. My thoughts have been informed and reshaped by the most enduring experience in my life: working with my patients. Many of the tenets in the book, especially those pertinent to making one's life easier, were developed during conversations with my patients, both otrovert and communal. I witnessed the salient difference between a life of belonging and a life of outsiders. I endeavored to find solutions to what bothered each patient. I became adept at seeing the world of my patient without judgment or preconceived notions; in other words, without my partialities interfering with my capacity for empathy. In a way, I have lived many lives seeing the world through my patients' eyes. Over the years, my patients have gifted me a multifaceted, nuanced understanding of humanity. Without them, this book would not have been possible. I am and have always been deeply grateful to my patients.

I want to thank those who literally made this book possible: Beth Davey, my outstanding and dedicated literary agent, and Talia Krohn, my fantastic and brilliant publisher and editor. They really "got it" and helped me polish my thoughts and infuse my voice into the text. I am very fortunate to have met Beth and Talia. With wisdom and kindness, they helped me enter the unfamiliar publishing world and come out on the other side wanting to write more.

There are many supportive people I met along the way who are not my patients; thus, I allow myself to acknowledge them by name: Melanie Rehak, Lindsay Taylor, Amy Phelan, Mimi Sternlicht, Amy Jurkowitz, Faina Shmulyian, James Stone, Joan Shanebrook, Yehuda Pearl, Joseph Shpigel, and Eli Meltzman.

Lastly, I want to acknowledge my first and most important teacher in psychiatry, Dr. Kallman. I learned everything I know about being an otrovert psychiatrist by watching him with patients and listening to him share his thoughts with me. How long would it have taken me to find my groove had he not put my feet on the ground? Dr. Kallman, if there is an otrovert's heaven, knowing you, you must have given your well-deserved place to one of your patients or students. I am eternally grateful to you.

Index

Index

About the Author

RAMI KAMINSKI, MD, is a pioneering psychiatrist with more than four decades of experience treating patients across the spectrum, from world leaders to individuals with persistent psychiatric conditions. His expertise includes mood disorders, obsessive-compulsive disorders, anxiety, addiction disorders, and neurocognitive conditions. With a particular focus on integrative psychiatric approaches, Dr. Kaminski's method uniquely bridges humanistic values with innovative therapeutic concepts.

Based in New York City, Dr. Kaminski continues to advance healthcare through optimized treatment protocols, with recent pioneering work in addiction treatment. His contributions to mental health include the development of the F.A.M.E. (Forecast, Assess, Manage, Empower) protocol, designed to address the psychological challenges of sudden fame, in 2018. In 2023, he founded the Otherness Institute, where he introduced the Otherness Scale—a method for identifying and measuring traits of otherness and otroversion.

During his tenure at Mount Sinai Medical Center, Dr. Kaminski made a discovery about histamine's role in degenerative brain disorders, leading to eleven international patents.

In the public sector, Dr. Kaminski served as medical director for operations and commissioner liaison to families at the New York State Office of Mental Health, where he implemented several innovative programs. Notable among these is the Second Chance Program, which has gained international recognition for its exceptional outcomes.

Dr. Kaminski's outstanding contributions to psychiatry have earned numerous accolades, including the Exemplary Psychiatrist Award from the National Alliance for the Mentally Ill and Mount Sinai Hospital's Physician of the Year award. As director of psychiatric medical students' education at Mount Sinai School of Medicine, he was awarded the Excellence in Service Award and inducted into the Medical Honor Society Alpha Omega Alpha, cementing his legacy as both a practitioner and an educator in the field of psychiatry.